EXCEL 2021

A Complete Guide on How to Use Excel in
General and All the Major Feature Updates
Related To the Latest Version of Excel

MAXWELL RUELL

Contents

Introduction

Microsoft Excel is a spreadsheet program for Windows, macOS, Android, and iOS that was created by Microsoft. It's a spreadsheet application for recording and analyzing numerical data. Consider a spreadsheet to be a table made up of columns and rows. Microsoft Corporation created MS excel in 1985. It helps in organizing data in rows and columns that can be modified using a formula to perform mathematical operations on the data.

This spreadsheet-based software tool developed by Microsoft employs formulas and functions to organize numbers and data. Excel analysis is used by advanced businesses of all sizes all over the world to execute the financial analysis. Excel has alleviated more pains than any pain medicine, and the world owes Microsoft a debt of gratitude for its invention. In this book, you will learn almost everything about Microsoft Excel and especially about the new features of Excel 2021, which is meant to assist users in computing different functions and formulas, has a variety of useful features. The mathematical calculations, on the other hand, allow users to assess large data sets with only a few basic settings. Users may quickly handle income statements, balance sheets, and other financial information sets using the formulas. Excel, like any other Microsoft product, is very simple to use. The design seems to readily direct novice users to the needed functionality, which is all neatly organized in a toolbar at the top of the screen. Individuals trying to handle social data will find the application incredibly useful. Users may add data for descriptions and titles in an infinite number of rows and columns, which can then be searched using a search option. Of course, users may use the software as a calendar of social events for their forthcoming activities at a most basic level. After all, no other software rival provides such a seamless experience with so many extra options. There is no better spreadsheet application than Microsoft Excel when it refers to spreadsheet computing.

Microsoft Excel was originally released on the market in 1987, 32 years ago. It was built as new software to calculate fundamental end-user functions for individuals searching for a faster way to compute. Many versions of MS excel have been launched, and the latest one is Excel 2021, which has highly professional features for high-end businesses and financial analysts to manage their work most efficiently like never before. The program grew increasingly sustainable over time for a variety of reasons. Users will be able to handle massive amounts of data, create balance sheets, and plan journeys in no time. Microsoft Excel nowadays provides so much more than that, allowing users to execute a number of spreadsheet-related activities. Those that open Excel will be able to get started using it right away. The user interface is divided into cells and comprises an unlimited number of columns and rows. Data becomes the part of the spreadsheet that is entered into a cell, which may be used for basic data storage or computations. The best part is that MS Excel spreadsheets are really simple to share and change. They may be shared quickly through email, external hard disc, or USB.

Forget about all of the hassles that come with bulk data input. Get started with Microsoft Excel to see how simple it is to create stunning spreadsheets. To remain competitive in today's environment, all businesses must adapt and progress. Implementing development programs so that workers can remain on top of the newest technology and work as effectively as possible is one approach to remain ahead of the pack and enhance profitability. Employers may also preserve one of their most significant assets: their people via ongoing training and growth. MS Excel helps the employees that are talented and desire to be motivated and work hard to remain ahead of the competition who must have the advanced knowledge of new software and technologies. Organizations can improve retention and lower employee turnover by giving them the education and training about the new coming advanced software such as Microsoft Excel to be as efficient as they want to be. They can also reduce to loss of valuable and the most talented employees to competitors by offering them ongoing training to be successful. Microsoft Excel for Business is an application that is often used in these business training programs. This book will teach you how to utilize Excel to better and effectively run your business.

Chapter 1: Introduction to Microsoft Excel

Microsoft Excel is among the most widely used software programs in the world. Microsoft Excel is used by thousands of millions of individuals all around the globe. Excel allows you to input a wide range of data and conduct financial, mathematical, and statistical computations. MS Excel is a spreadsheet tool that is part of the Microsoft Office suite. Spreadsheets are rows and columns of numbers that may be changed numerically using both simple and advanced arithmetic functions and operations. The application is compatible with a variety of operating systems, including Windows, tablets, mac-OS, and smartphones.

1.1 What Is Excel?

Microsoft Excel is a useful and sophisticated software for documentation and data analysis. It's a spreadsheet application with several columns and rows, with each junction of a row and a column being referred to as a "cell." Each cell includes a single piece of data or information. You may make information simpler to access and automatically derive info from changing data by arranging the data in this manner. It is a tool developed by Microsoft that enables users to organize, arrange, and compute data using formulae. This program is included in the MS Office suite, which is compatible with other Office programs. Microsoft Excel, like other Office applications, is available as a cloud-based subscription via Office 365.

Microsoft Excel is a commercial spreadsheet tool developed by Microsoft and published for the Mac OS operating systems and Microsoft Windows. It includes, among other things, the ability to make simple calculations, utilize graphing tools, construct pivot tables, and construct macros. To organize and manage data, spreadsheet programs like MS Excel employ a collection of cells organized into rows and columns. They can also use charts, histograms, and line graphs to present data. MS Excel allows users to organize information in order to see various elements from multiple angles. Excel has a programming language called the Microsoft Visual basic that may be used to develop a range of advanced numerical algorithms in Excel. Programmers have the option of creating code directly in the Visual Basic Editor, which includes Windows for debugging and organizing code modules. Microsoft Excel played a critical role in accounting and record-keeping for company operations in the early years of accessible business computing. Table with an AutoSum format is one of the greatest examples of an MS Excel use case. Entering a column of data and clicking into the cell at the bottom of the excel spreadsheet, then using the "AutoSum" button to enable that cell to add all of the numbers up in the input above, is fairly simple with Microsoft Excel. This replaces manual ledger counts, which were a time-consuming component of business prior to the development of the current spreadsheet. MS Excel has become a must-have for numerous types of corporate computing, which includes looking at daily, weekly, or monthly data, tabulating taxes and payroll, and other comparable corporate procedures, thanks to the AutoSum and other developments.

Microsoft Excel has become a crucial end-user technology, valuable in professional development and training, thanks to a variety of easy application cases. MS Excel has been added in courses of basic business diploma on business computers for a number of years, and temporary job agencies may evaluate persons for a variety of clerical roles based on their capabilities with Microsoft Excel.

1.2 Brief History of Microsoft

In 1975, two boyhood friends from Seattle, Paul G. Allen and Bill Gates, modified BASIC, a famous programming language of a mainframe computer, to use on the Altair, an old personal computer. Allen and Gates and launched Microsoft not long after, naming it after the phrases software and microcomputer. They improved BASIC and created new programming languages over the following several years. In 1980, IBM requested Microsoft to provide the key operating system or software for the IBM PC, which was the company's very 1st PC. Microsoft bought another company's operating system, changed it. They renamed it MS Disk Operating System (MS-DOS). In 1981, Microsoft-DOS was launched alongside the IBM Personal Computer. Following that, most personal computer manufacturers licensed the new MS Disk Operating System as their leading operating system, producing massive revenues for Microsoft Corporation; Around the early months of 1990s, there were over millions of copies of this software that were sold, defeating rival systems like CP/M. With a graphical and friendly user interface, with Windows, whose third edition is introduced in 1990, Microsoft established its stronghold in operating systems. Millions of copies of The Windows 3.0 version and other later versions were sold out on monthly basis, and Microsoft's operating system was installed on roughly 90% of the world's computers. Around 1995, Company developed

Windows 95 that completely merged new operating system of Microsoft with Windows for the first time and essentially equaled Apple Computer's Mac OS in terms of simplicity of use. Microsoft also surpassed long-time competitors Lotus and WordPerfect as the top seller in productivity apps like word processors and spreadsheet tools.

1.3 History of MS Excel

Microsoft is a company that specializes in Excel that has been around since 1982 when it was initially released as Multiplan, a spreadsheet program that was very successful on CP/M systems but lost ground to Lotus 1-2-3 on MS-DOS systems. It was a popular Control Program for Microcomputers (CP/M), but when Lotus 1-2-3 quickly overtook it on MS-DOS systems, it prompted the creation of a brand new spreadsheet known as Excel, which was created with the goal of "doing everything 1-2-3 does, but better."

Microsoft released Excel v2.0 for Windows in 1987, and by 1988, it had begun to outsell the famous Lotus 1-2-3 and the nascent Quatro-Pro. Visual Basic for Applications VBA), often known as Macros, was featured in Microsoft Excel 5.0 for Windows in 1993. This opened up almost limitless possibilities in terms of automating repetitive operations like number crunching, process automation, and data presentation for enterprises. Lotus 1-2-3, initially released in 1982 by the Lotus Development Corporation, dominated the early 1980s spreadsheet industry for personal computers (PCs) running Microsoft's MS-DOS operating system. Microsoft created a rival spreadsheet, and the very first version of MS Excel for Apple Inc.'s Macintosh computer was published in 1985. The new program soon gained popularity due to its excellent visuals and speedy processing. Excel was able to establish popularity among Macintosh users since Lotus 1-2-3 was not supported for the Macintosh. In 1987, Microsoft released the next version of Excel, which was the first to operate on the company's new Windows operating system. The powerful application gained popularity because of its graphics-heavy interface, which was built to operate on the newest Windows systems. Lotus took a long time to create a Version for windows of its spreadsheet, enabling Excel to gain market dominance and finally overtake Lotus as the most popular spreadsheet program in the mid-1990s. Excel had begun to outsell 1-2-3, assisting Microsoft in becoming the major PC software developer. Toolbars, drawing, outlining, and 3-D charts, various shortcuts, and much more automated functions were all included in later versions of Excel. Microsoft updated the naming scheme for Excel in 1995 to highlight the product's first release year. Excel 95 was created for the newest Intel Corporation 386 microprocessor-based 32-bit systems. Microsoft maintained its lead by releasing new software every two years or so.

In 1997 Excel 97 and in 1999 Excel 2000, these new versions were released. Excel 2002 was introduced in 2003 as part of the Office XP package, and it introduced a major new feature that enabled users to restore Excel data and files in the case of a computer breakdown. Excel 2007 included a revamped user interface that shared functionality with Microsoft's Word and PowerPoint programs, enabling users to navigate seamlessly between them. Additionally, chart creation, security, data sharing, formula writing, filtering and sorting have all been enhanced. This achievement, which dethroned the monarch of the software business, established Microsoft as a legitimate contender and demonstrated its commitment to producing graphical software in the future.

Present Day Microsoft Excel

Due to its flexibility to adapt to practically any business activity, Microsoft Excel is one of the most familiar, adaptable, and frequently used the business program in the world today, including the newest releases of Excel 2021 and Excel365. When used in conjunction with other Microsoft Office apps such as Word, Outlook, and PowerPoint, there is very nothing that this strong combo cannot manage.

The Future of Excel

What are the options now? With the internet playing such an important role in your lives and businesses, it's only natural that the demands of the many would win out. Staying current on upcoming technologies has become a full-time job as Microsoft systems continue to change. Microsoft Excel will continue to be the most popular platform for analyzing data, creating presentations and charts, and integrating with sophisticated tools for business intelligence workflows and visual dashboards.

Businesses are increasingly turning to cloud computing for data accessibility and collaboration. It envisions Microsoft Excel's future in the next several years growing at a break-neck pace to enable multi-user access to large data for reporting, analysis, and significant advances in efficiency and productivity. Custom solutions are necessary for today's competitive corporate climate to preserve a competitive advantage and maximize profitability. Microsoft Excel consulting firms are the best knowledgeable about current and new technology. Having a retained professional consultant is critical in achieving the full efficiency required to succeed in the twenty-first century.

1.4 How to Get Started With MS Excel?

To begin using Microsoft Excel, you must first install it on your computer, phone, or other Android or iOS device. While MS Excel for PCs can only be obtained as part of the MS Office suite, Excel for iPhone and Android may be downloaded for free. Keep in mind that in order to purchase and to use Office 365 on your computer, you'll need to have a Microsoft account.

1. **Using Office 365 on Desktop:** Buy an Office 365 subscription. You'll need to acquire an Office 365 subscription before you can access Microsoft Excel for long-term usage. Instead, you may find a free trial of Office 365 and download it to check it out for a month.

2. **Office 365 Installation on Your Device:** Go to the Office section of your account.

- In your computer's web browser, open the website of your 'my account' for office.

- If you're logged in, this will take you to your Office subscription page.

- If asked, add your email address with a password if you aren't already signed in. Then Install it. On the left of the website, there's an orange button for install.

- When you click it, the Office setup file will begin to download. Before the file begins downloading, you may need to pick a save place or confirm the download based on your browser's settings.

- Install Office 365 now. This step will vary based on your computer's operating system. Do the following after double-clicking the Office setup file:

For Mac — Select the Continue button and then click Agree. Now again, select Continue and then install. Enter the password of your Mac system and click Install Software, then close when it appears.

For Windows — Select the Yes button when prompted, and then wait for Office 365 to complete the installation. Now you'll have to click close and finalize the installation.

Now the Microsoft Excel will be installed as part of each version of Office 365, and you'll find it once the installation process completes:

For Mac — Select the Spotlight button and then type 'Excel' to bring the Excel in the search results at the top.

For Windows — Select the Start button and then type 'Excel' to bring the Excel icon as the first one in the Start menu.

3. Using a Free Trial on Desktop:

Go to the free trial page of the Office to get started. In your computer's web browser, type https://products.office.com/en-us/try. If you download the Office 365 free trial, you may use Excel for a month free.

- Select the Free 1-Month Trial option. It's on the page's left side.

- When asked, log in to your Microsoft account. To do so, give your email address with your password. This step may not be necessary if you recently logged into your Microsoft account.

- Select the next option. Towards the end of the page, you'll find it.

- Decide on a mode of payment. Under the "Pick a payment method" section, input your card information, click debit card or credit card, or pick other alternatives (e.g., PayPal) section. While you won't be charged for Office 365 right away, you will be charged for one year after your one-month trial period has ended.

- Fill in the payment details for the payment type you've chosen. This will contain your card number, card expiry date, and other information for a card. If you choose a payment option other than a credit card, you'll need to enter your information using the on-screen instructions.

- Go to the bottom of the page and choose the next option. This will bring you to the overview page. If you paid using a means other than a credit card, you might be asked to provide your billing information and select next before proceeding.

- Next, choose the option to subscribe. This option could be found at the end of the page. After that, you'll be brought to the account's "Office" page.

- Get Office 365 and install it. Perform the following actions:

- Select Install on the left of the page.

- Double-click the downloaded Office 365 setup file.

- Follow any installation steps that appear on the screen.

- Before you're charged, cancel your trial. If you don't like to be charged for a year in a month's time, take these steps:

- If you want to cancel, then go to your Microsoft account and log in.

- Under the "Office 365" header, scroll down and choose Payment & billing.

- A page will appear; on the right side, click Cancel and when requested, click Confirm cancellation.

On iPhone: Open the App Store on your iPhone.

- Click the search box.

- Look for Excel on the internet. Type excel into the search box, then hit excel from the list of results. This will open the Excel spreadsheet.

- Select "Get" from the drop-down menu. It's directly next to the Excel icon. If you've already downloaded Excel, press the "Download" icon instead.

- Put in your Touch ID code. To be sure you've made the right selection, scan your fingerprint. The download of Microsoft Excel will begin.

- Once downloaded, you can use Excel on your iPhone.

On Android: Open the Google Play Store on your Android device.

- Click on the search bar if your Play Store displays a different tab than GAMES, press GAMES towards the top right of your screen before tapping the search field.

- Type excel, then choose Microsoft Excel from the drop-down options. You'll be sent to the MS Excel page as a result of this.

- Select the option to install. It will begin to download Microsoft Excel. To begin the download, hit ACCEPT if requested.

- Once downloaded, you can use excel on your android device.

1.5 Main Parts of MS Excel

You can use excel to do computations, analyses, and visualizations of information and data once you have it downloaded on your device. For documentation and data analysis, Excel is useful and sophisticated software. A spreadsheet software with several columns and rows, with each crossing between a column and a row being referred to as a "cell." Each cell includes a single piece of data or information. You may make information simpler to access and automatically derive information by changing data and arranging the data in this manner. To perform all of this, you must first understand the fundamentals of Excel. The primary elements of practically all current versions of MS Excel that include Office 365, Excel 2021, Excel 2019, 2016, and other previous versions, are listed here. There may be some minor variations, but these versions are quite comparable.

The Excel Start Screen: The Microsoft Excel Start Screen appears when you launch Excel for the very first time. You can choose a template or create a new workbook and retrieve your recently changed workbooks from here. Locate and choose Blank workbook from the MS Excel Start Screen to enter the Excel interface.

Spreadsheet Basics: Each MS Excel file is a workbook, and each workbook may include several worksheets. The worksheet consists of rows and columns. The blue buttons at the top of the worksheet identify the letters of the columns. The row numbers are given by the blue buttons on the worksheet's left side. A cell is the point where a row a column and meet. You may fill in the blanks with your information. Text, numbers, and formulas for automated computations may all be entered into cells. The cell address for each cell in the spreadsheet is the column letter accompanied by the row number.

The Parts of The Excel Window: Some features of the excel window, are common in most Microsoft programs. The formula bar, worksheet and name box tabs, on the other hand, are more spreadsheet-specific features. The various components of the Excel window are as follows:

1. **Quick Access Toolbar:** Regardless of whatever tab is chosen, the Quick Access Toolbar allows you to access popular tasks. You may personalize the instructions to suit your needs.

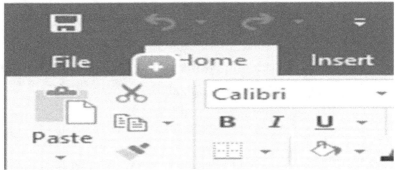

2. **The Ribbon:** The Ribbon provides all of the instructions that you'll need to do typical Excel operations. It features various tabs, each with a different set of instructions.

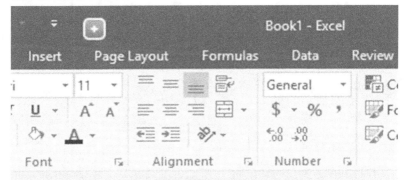

3. **Tell me:** The Tell me option functions similarly to a search bar, allowing you to easily locate tools or instructions.

4. **Name Box:** The Name box option shows the name, or location, of the chosen cell.

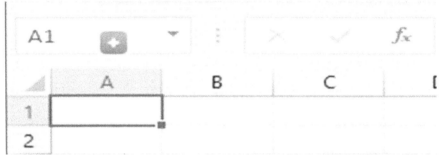

5. **Microsoft Account:** You can browse your profile, switch accounts, and manage your MS account information from here.

6. Formula Bar: You can input or change data, a function, a formula that will show in a particular cell in the formula bar.

7. Cell: A cell is a rectangular area in a workbook. A cell is a point where a column a row and meet. To choose a cell, just click it.

Cell Address: The name that may be used to address a cell is called the cell address. If row 7 is inserted in column G, for example, the cell address will be G7.

8. Column: A column is a set of cells that runs from top to bottom on a page. Columns in Excel are denoted by letters.

9. **Row:** A row is a set of cells that runs from left to right across the page. Numbers are used to identifying rows in Excel.

10. **Worksheets**: Workbooks are the name given to Excel files. Worksheets are included in each workbook. To switch between tabs, click them, or you can right-click on them for additional choices.

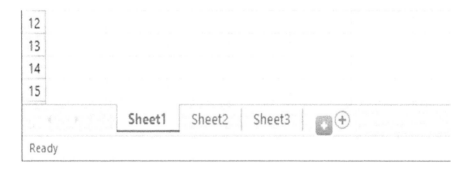

11. **Worksheet View Options:** To view the worksheet, here are 3 ways. You can simply click on this command and select the view that you desire.

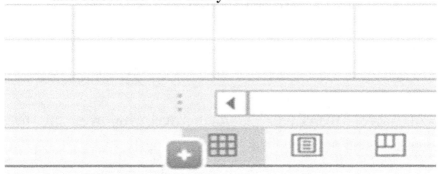

12. **Vertical and Horizontal Scroll Bars:** You can scroll up and down or side to side using the scroll bars. To do so, hover your mouse over the horizontal or vertical scroll bar and drag it up or down.

13. **Zoom Control:** To utilize the zoom control, click and move the slider. The zoom percentage is shown by the number written on the right of the slider.

Full Excel Interface: The main Excel window or interface comprises all the previously mentioned parts.

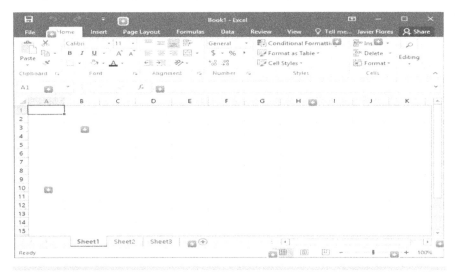

1.6 Working with the Excel Environment

To work with Excel, you need to first understand the working of all the major parts of the excel window, which includes the excel interface as well as the Backstage view. The controls to conduct common actions in Excel may be found on Quick Access Toolbar and the Ribbon. The Backstage view provides you with a variety of choices for saving, printing, viewing, and sharing your work.

1. **The Ribbon:** Instead of typical menus, Excel has a tabbed Ribbon structure. The Ribbon has various tabs, each with a different set of instructions. These tabs will help you accomplish the most frequent Excel activities.

- There will be one or more groups on each tab.

- You'll see an arrow next to certain groupings that you may click to see additional possibilities.

- To view additional commands, choose a tab.

- The Ribbon Display menu Options allow you to customize how the Ribbon is presented.

- Extra tabs to the Ribbon may be installed by certain apps, for example, Adobe Acrobat Reader. Add-ins are the name for these tabs.

To Change The Ribbon Display Options: The Ribbon is meant to adapt to your current project, but if it occupies too much screen space, you can opt to minimize it. To access the drop-down menu, click on the options of Ribbon Display that is on the upper-right corner of the Ribbon. In the options menu of Ribbon, there are three options to choose from:

- **Auto-hide Ribbon:** It covers the Ribbon and puts your worksheet in full-screen mode. Select the Expand Ribbon option at the top of the screen to see the Ribbon.

- **Show Tabs:** When not in use, this option covers all command groups, but tabs remain visible. Simply press a tab to bring up the Ribbon.

- **Show Tabs and Commands:** It is the option that expands the Ribbon to its full potential. You'll be able to see all of the instructions and tabs. When you launch MS Excel for the first time, this option is chosen by default.

2. **The Quick Access Toolbar:** The Quick Access Toolbar, which is located right above the Ribbon, allows you to access common actions regardless of which tab is chosen. It comes with the Undo, Save, and Repeats commands by default. Depending on your preferences, you may add other commands.

To add other options/commands to the Quick Access Toolbar:

- On the right of the Quick Access Toolbar, click the drop-down arrow.

- From the drop-down menu, choose the command you wish to add. Select More Commands to get a list of more commands.

- In the Quick Access Toolbar, the commands will be added

3. **Tell Me:** The Tell me box functions similarly to a search bar, allowing you to easily locate tools or instructions.

- Write out what you want to accomplish in your own words.

- You'll have a few alternatives based on the findings. To utilize one, click it as if it were a Ribbon command.

4. **Worksheet Views:** Excel provides a number of different viewing settings that change the appearance of your worksheet. These views are useful for a variety of activities, particularly if you want to print your spreadsheet.

Select Page Layout view, Normal view, or Page Break view from the instructions, which is present at the right corner at the bottom of the Excel window to change worksheet views.

- Page Layout view shows how the worksheets will look when printed.

- The default view is the Normal view which is for all of the worksheets in Excel. In this mode, you may also include headers and footers.

- The Page Break view enables you to move page breaks around, which is extremely useful when printing a large amount of data from Excel.

5. **Backstage view:** Backstage view provides a variety of choices for saving, viewing, sharing and printing workbooks.

To access Back-stage view: Click on the **File** tab at the top of the excel window on the **Ribbon**. It will take you to the **backstage view.**

All the options of backstage view from top to bottom are as follows:

- **Return to Excel**: You can use this arrow option to close the Back-stage view and then return to the Excel window.

- **Info:** You will see the Info pane option whenever you will come to the Back-stage view. It contains all the information that belongs to your current workbook.

- **New:** From this option, you can make a blank new workbook, or you can select from a large number of templates.

- **Open:** From this option, you can always open a recently done workbook and also the workbooks that are saved in your One-Drive or that are present on your personal computer.

- **Save and Save As**: Use this option to save your current workbook on your computer, or you can also save it to your One-Drive.

- **Print**: From the Print pane option, you can easily alter the settings of print for your workbook. Preview of your workbook can also be seen using this option.

- **Share**: Using this option, you can send an invitation to the people to see and collaborate on the workbook you have just completed. You can share it with other people by emailing them the workbook as an attachment.

- **Export**: You can export your workbook if you wish in different formats, such as Excel 1997-2021 or PDF/XPS using this option.

- **Publish**: Using this option, you can easily publish the workbook to Microsoft's cloud-sharing option for MS Excel workbooks or Power BI.

- **Close**: Click this option to close your current workbook.

- **Account**: From the Account pane option, you can use your MS account info, modify your background and theme, and can sign out of your Microsoft account.

- **Options**: Using this, you can always change various types of Excel settings, options, and preferences for language.

Chapter 2: Overview of All Uses of Microsoft Excel

Excel is often used for data organization and financial analysis. It is utilized in all business operations and by businesses of all sizes. MS Excel is commonly used these days by everyone since it is incredibly useful and saves a lot of time. It has been in use for many years and is improved with new features every year. MS Excel's most striking feature is that it could be utilized anywhere and for any type of work. It is utilized for things like billing, analysis, data management, inventory, business duties, finance and sophisticated computations, among other things. It may also be used to do mathematical computations and to store critical data in the form of spreadsheets or charts.

The office Suite and Microsoft Excel have almost infinite applications. Take a look at the following list of the most popular and useful Excel features. The following are some of Excel's most common uses:

- Data management

- Accounting

- Data Entry

- Financial analysis

- Programming

- Graphing and charting and

- Management of tasks

- Management of time

- Customer relationship management (CRM)

- Financial modeling

It organizes anything which needs to get organized and managed.

- Model and analyses practically any data efficiently

- Quickly zero in on the correct data points

- Create data visualizations in a one cell

- Take benefit of more dynamic and interactive Pivot Charts

- You can use your spreadsheets from anywhere virtually.

- Add more elegance to your presentations

- Make things simpler and quicker

- Harness greater power for generating larger, more complicated spreadsheets

- Work together to connect, share, and achieve more

- Excel Services allows you to publish and share your work.

When you combine all of the above with the ability to modify and automate any activity using Visual Basic for Applications (VBA), you have a powerful Business Intelligence (BI) platform that is versatile and innovative enough to address practically any business requirement. MS Excel protects your files, ensuring that nobody else may access or corrupt them. You may password-protect your files with the aid of MS Excel. MS Excel is accessible from any location and at any time. If you don't have access to a laptop, you may use your phone to work on MS Excel. MS Excel has so many advantages that it is becoming an unavoidable part of millions of people's lives. MS Excel provides a variety of features and tools that make work easier and save time.

To get the most out of MS Excel, you must first understand how it works. The following are the most in-depth uses of Microsoft Excel:

2.1 Storing and Analyzing Data

One of the most useful features of Microsoft Excel is the ability to analyses vast volumes of data in order to spot patterns. You may summarize data and save it in an orderly manner with the aid of charts and graphs and so that you can readily access it whenever you need it. It becomes easy to save data, and you will save a great amount of time as a result. Data may be utilized for a variety of reasons after it has been saved in a systematic manner. Excel makes it much easier to do numerous operations on data by providing a variety of tools.

2.2 Excel Tools That Make Your Work Much Easier

MS Excel has a variety of functions that make your job a lot easier and save you time. There are fantastic tools for filtering, sorting, and searching that make your job even easier. You can do your task in much less time if you utilize these tools with pivot tables and other tools. Multiple items may be quickly searched from enormous volumes of data to assist in the solution of a variety of issues and concerns.

2.3 Spreadsheets and Data Recovery

Another advantageous feature of Microsoft Excel is for your lost data that if your data gets deleted or lost, you may easily retrieve it. If a businessman has essential data recorded in MS Excel and it is destroyed lost, or the file is lost, he need not worry since the new Excel XML format may be used to recover the damaged file lost or data. The second key purpose is that MS Excel spreadsheets make your job easier, and you may minimize the size of your spreadsheet and make things small simply using the new Microsoft Excel XML format.

2.4 Mathematical Formulas That Make Calculation Easier

The next great use of Excel is that it allows you to tackle complicated mathematical issues in a much easier and less time-consuming manner. There are numerous formulas in MS Excel, and by utilizing them, you can do a variety of operations on a huge quantity of data at once, such as computing the sum, average, and so on. As a result, MS Excel is used anytime users need to solve difficult mathematical issues or apply basic mathematical functions to tables with a lot of data.

2.5 Security

The most important feature of Microsoft Excel is that it secures Excel files, allowing users to keep their data safe. Directly inside the excel file or through Visual Basic programming, all MS Excel files can be password-protected. People maintain their vital data in Excel so that they may keep it structured and save time. Almost everyone wants their files to just be password secured so that nobody can access them or damage them, and MS Excel is an excellent solution to this issue.

2.6 Add Sophistication to Your Data Presentations

The next benefit of MS Excel is that it allows you to add more elegance to your data presentations, which means you can enhance the data bars, highlight any particular elements you want to emphasize, and quickly make your data more attractive. If you have data saved in Excel and you desire to emphasize something significant, you can do it using the numerous data presentation options provided in MS Excel. You can even modify the spreadsheets on which you've placed data more appealing.

2.7 Accessible Online

Another advantage of Excel is that it is accessible from anywhere, online and at any time, allowing you to utilize it from any place and from any device. It allows you to work more conveniently, which implies that if you don't have a laptop, you may use your phone to do your tasks quickly and effortlessly. As a result of the extensive versatility that MS Excel offers, individuals choose to work on it so that they may focus on their job without being distracted by their location or device.

2.8 Keeps Your Data Combined At One Place

Another useful feature of Excel is that it allows you to store all of your data in one place. This will assist you in preventing the loss of your data. It will preserve all of your stuff in one location, so you won't have to spend time looking for files. As a result, you will save time and will be able to conveniently seek up the classified and sorted data whenever you need it.

2.9 Helps Businessmen in Making Future Strategy

Data may be represented in the form of graphs and charts to aid in the identification of various trends. Trend lines may be stretched outside the graph with the aid of MS Excel, making it simpler to analyses patterns and trends. In order to improve sales, it is essential to examine the selling strategy that they follow or the popularity of items. MS Excel makes this work easier for company owners, allowing them to expand and maximize revenues.

2.10 Manage Expenses

MS Excel is useful for budgeting. For example, if a doctor earns $50,000 per month, he will spend a certain amount on expenses, and if he desires to know precisely how much he is spending each month, he may simply do so using MS Excel. He may enter his monthly income and costs into excel tables, which will allow him to see how much income he is spending and, as a result, reduce his spending.

There are several advantages to utilizing Excel, which is why it is utilized by people all over the globe for a variety of jobs. Not only does it save time, but it also makes the job simpler. It is virtually capable of completing any work. For example, you may do mathematical computations as well as create graphs and charts to save data. It is simple for a businessperson to compute and save data in it. MS Excel has the ability to store and analyses massive amounts of data. It helps to maintain all of the data in one location so that nothing is lost and no time is wasted looking for specific information. It has become a popular program as a result of these features, and you will get used to using it.

2.11 Some Other Captivating Uses of MS Excel

Excel is becoming the professional standard in businesses throughout the world for just about everything that involves the administration of huge volumes of data, with more than 1 billion Microsoft Office users worldwide. Think again if you think MS Excel is just excellent for making you less worried when staring at a lot of figures and financial reports. Outside just basic spreadsheets, there are a number of applications for Excel in managing your business (and beyond), as Tomasz Tunguz demonstrates out. In fact, the possible applications seem to be limitless. In order to showcase the power and versatility of everyone's favorite spreadsheet program, we've compiled a list of numerous ways you may utilize Excel both professionally and personally, as well as simply for fun.

1. All About Numbers

Of course, Excel's main function is to work with numbers. Excel makes sorting, retrieving, and analyzing a huge (or even tiny!) quantity of data a breeze. When it comes to using Excel for anything numbers-related, there are a few general categories to keep in mind.

- **Calculating:** Simple formulas may be entered to add, subtract, divide, or multiply two or more numbers. Alternatively, you may use the AutoSum tool to instantly sum a set of numbers without having to manually input them into a formula. You may replicate a formula into neighboring cells once you've created it; there's no need to repeat the process. By programming your frequently used formulae in Excel, you may create a completely personalized calculator. That way, all you have to do is punch in your figures, and MS Excel will spit out the result for you with no effort on your part. You can easily multiply, divide, add, and subtract your data with Excel. To imitate a calculator, just enter basic formulas in the formula bar. The equal symbol (=) appears at the start of every formula entry. Simply write the equal symbol followed by the numeric numbers to compute and the arithmetic operators to utilize to subtract, the minus sign (-), the plus symbol (+) to add, the slash (/) to divide, and to multiply use the asterisk (*) for basic formulas. Then hit ENTER, and Excel calculates and shows the formula's output right away. When you input =12.99+16.99 in cell C5 and hit the ENTER, MS Excel calculates the answer and shows 29.98. When you input a formula in a cell, it stays displayed in the formula bar and is displayed anytime that cell is chosen.

Note: There is no subtract function, despite the fact that there is a sum function. For subtracting, in a formula, use the negative (-) operator; for example, =8-3+2-4+12. Alternatively, you may use a minus (-) sign in the Sum function to transform a quantity to its negative value; the formula =SUM(12,5,-3,8,-4) for example, employs the Sum function to add 12 and 5, remove 3, add 8, and then subtract 4 in that sequence.

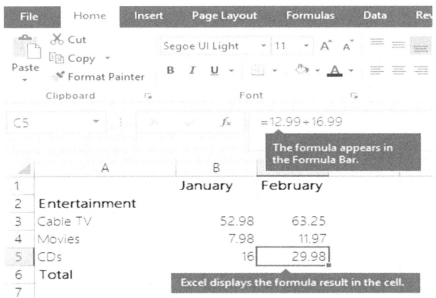

- **Use of AutoSum:** AutoSum is the simplest method to add a SUM calculation to your spreadsheet. Select an unfilled cell just below or above the range you wish to sum, then select AutoSum on the Formula tabs or Home of the ribbon. AutoSum will detect the range to be added and construct the sum formula for you. If you choose a cell to the right or left of the range to sum, this also works horizontally.

Note: Non-contiguous ranges are not supported by AutoSum.

- **Avoid Rewriting the Same Formula:** You can duplicate a formula to other cells after you've created it, so you don't have to redo it. You have the option of copying the formula or using the fill handle to duplicate it to neighboring cells. When you duplicate the formula from cell B6 to cell C6, for example, the formula in the cell changes the cell references to reflect in column C. Make sure the cell references are right when copying the formula. If relative references are used, cell references may vary.

- **Accounting**: Budgeting, forecasting, cost monitoring, loan calculators, financial reports, and other tools are all available. Excel was essentially created to fulfill these various accounting requirements. And, given that 89 % use Excel for different accounting duties, it clearly meets the criteria. Excel even comes with a variety of spreadsheet templates to help you with all of these tasks.

COMPANY XYZ

REVENUES	OPERATING PROFIT	EXPENSE	DEPRECIATION	NET PROFIT
$180,584	$73,426	$3,789	$5,547	$67,475

- **Charting**: The collection of scatter charts, pie charts, line charts, area charts, bar charts, and column charts is endless. Excel's ability to turn columns and rows of figures into attractive charts is likely to be one of your favorite features if you need to convey data in a more consumable and visual manner.

Budget

% of Income Spent Summary

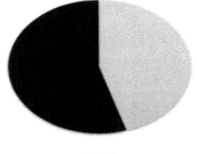

55%

Total Monthly Income
$3,750
Total Monthly Expenses
$2,058
Total Monthly Savings
$550
Cash Balance
$1,142

- **Inventory Tracking**: Inventory management can be a pain. Fortunately, Excel can assist workers, company owners, and even individuals in staying organized and at the peak of their inventory management before big issues arise.

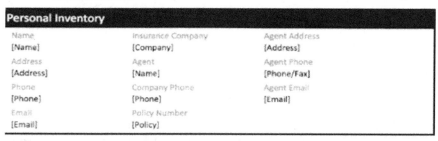

Personal Inventory		
Name	Insurance Company	Agent Address
[Name]	[Company]	[Address]
Address	Agent	Agent Phone
[Address]	[Name]	[Phone/Fax]
Phone	Company Phone	Agent Email
[Phone]	[Phone]	[Email]
Email	Policy Number	
[Email]	[Policy]	

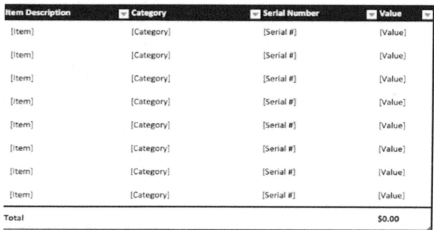

Item Description	Category	Serial Number	Value
[Item]	[Category]	[Serial #]	[Value]
[Item]	[Category]	[Serial #]	[Value]
[Item]	[Category]	[Serial #]	[Value]
[Item]	[Category]	[Serial #]	[Value]
[Item]	[Category]	[Serial #]	[Value]
[Item]	[Category]	[Serial #]	[Value]
[Item]	[Category]	[Serial #]	[Value]
[Item]	[Category]	[Serial #]	[Value]
Total			$0.00

2. **Making a Plan:** Let's get away from the numbers for a moment—Excel can help you organize and plan a lot of things that don't need endless rows of figures.

Daily Schedule

	Mon	Tue	Wed	Thu	Fri	Sat	Sun
5:00 AM	Go to gym						
5:30 AM							
6:00 AM							
6:30 AM							
7:00 AM							
7:30 AM							
8:00 AM							

- **Schedules and Calendars:** Do you need to create a content schedule for your website blog or? Are you looking for lesson ideas for your classroom? Is there a PTO that is scheduled for you and your coworkers? Do you and your family have a daily schedule? Excel may be surprisingly important with regard to multiple calendars.

Task	Times/Week	S	M	T	W	T	F	S	Complete
Go for a run	2	✔		✔					Yay!
Don't Leave Dirty Dishes Overnight	2	✔			✔		✔		Yay!
Eat 1 Fruit or Vegetable	3	✔			✔	✔	✔	✔	Yay!
Floss	3	✔		✔			✔	✔	Yay!

8-3-2014

Task	Times/Week	S	M	T	W	T	F	S	Complete
Go for a run	2								0 of 2
Don't Leave Dirty Dishes Overnight	3								0 of 3
Eat 1 Fruit or Vegetable	3								0 of 3
Floss	3								0 of 3

- **Seating Charts**: Creating a seating plan for anything from a major business lunch to a wedding may be a royal pain. Excel, fortunately, can turn it into a breeze. If you're clever enough, you'll be able to build your seating chart automatically from your RSVP spreadsheet.

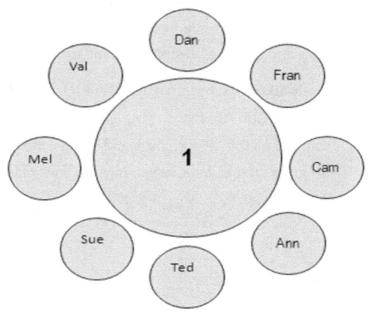

- **Goal planning worksheet:** Excel's beauty can be seen as it assists you in having something to keep you motivated and on track, whether it's career objectives, fitness goals. You may use the tool to build a variety of logs, spreadsheets, and planning papers to track your progress and, ideally, finish the race.

- **Mock-ups:** When it refers to the design, Excel may not be the only thing that springs to mind. However, believe it or not, the tool may be used to create numerous prototypes and mock-ups. It's a popular option for developing website wireframes and dashboards, in particular.

3. Getting Things Done

Do you want to increase your productivity? Excel, can come to your rescue with a range of functions that may help you manage your chores and to-dos with simplicity and order.

- **Task list:** Bye-bye to your traditional to-do list on paper. With MS Excel, you can create a far more comprehensive work list—and even monitor your progress on the big tasks you have on your plate.

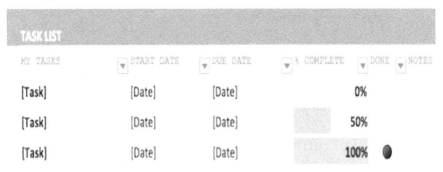

MY TASKS	START DATE	DUE DATE	% COMPLETE	DONE	NOTES
[Task]	[Date]	[Date]	0%		
[Task]	[Date]	[Date]	50%		
[Task]	[Date]	[Date]	100%	●	

- **Checklist:** You can make a basic checklist to cross off the items you've bought or completed from a shopping list to a list of to-dos for a planned marketing campaign.

PURCHASED?	GROCERIES:
☐	Apples
☑	Tomatoes
☐	Milk
☐	Eggs
☐	Cheese
☐	Bread

- **Project management charts:** Excel is a real beast in designing charts, as you have previously seen. This principle is also valid when it comes to different project management charts. Excel can help you keep the project on schedule in a variety of methods, from the waterfall charts to Kanab styled board to oversee your team's progress.

- **Time logs:** You already know that keeping track of your time may help you in being more productive. While there are many sophisticated applications and tools to assist you in satisfying that demand, consider MS Excel as the original time-tracking tool. It continues to be a viable alternative today.

Time Sheet

[Employee name] | [Email] | [Phone]
Manager | [Manager name]

Period [Start date] - [End date]

Standard Work Week	Hours Worked	Regular Hours	Overtime Hours
40.00	0.00	0.00	0.00

Date(s)	Time In	Lunch Start	Lunch End	Time Out	Hours Worked
[Date]	[Time In]	[Lunch Start]	[Lunch End]	[Time Out]	0.00
[Date]	[Time In]	[Lunch Start]	[Lunch End]	[Time Out]	0.00
[Date]	[Time In]	[Lunch Start]	[Lunch End]	[Time Out]	0.00
[Date]	[Time In]	[Lunch Start]	[Lunch End]	[Time Out]	0.00
[Date]	[Time In]	[Lunch Start]	[Lunch End]	[Time Out]	0.00

4. **Involving Other People:** Do you need to get information from others? One method is to use survey tools and forms. But, don't worry, you can make your own in Microsoft Excel.

- **Forms:** Excel is an excellent tool for designing forms, from basic to complex. You may even create numerous drop-down lists so that users may choose from a pre-defined list of options.

- **Quizzes:** Trying to assess someone else's or even your own understanding of a topic? You can generate a pool of questionnaires with answers in one worksheet and then make an Excel quiz you using those questions in another worksheet.

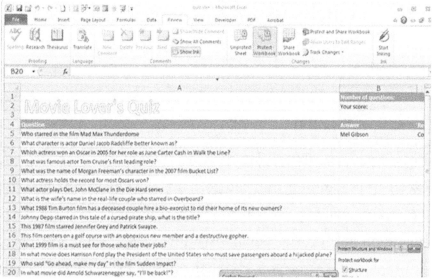

5. **Staying in Touch:** Relationship management is critical to your career and personal success. Excel, fortunately, makes it simple to stay in contact.

- **Customer Relationship Management software (CRM):** Do you need a simple CRM to remain top of mind with your customers? One may be created in Excel. The best part is that it will be completely customizable if you build it yourself.

CRM Template
[Your Name]

Name	Company	Work Function	Phone	Email	Estimated Sale	Last Contact	Next Action	Next Contact	Lead Status	Lead Source
Jameson, Bill	XYZ Plumbing	Owner	444 555 6666	mail@number.com	$ 45,000	1/10/13		1/29/13	Cold	Referral
Anderson, Jane	ABC Corp	Sales Manager	222 456 7890	mail@mail.com	$ 10,000	1/25/13		2/5/13	Warm	Website
Smithers, Joe	ACME	Business Dev	111 234 5678	mail@mail.com	$ 4,500	1/27/13		2/16/13	Active	Email

- **Mailing list**

Data does not always have to be numerical. Excel is also excellent at handling and categorizing huge lists of names and addresses, making it ideal for your company's holiday party invitation list or the email lists for a significant campaign or promotion. Also, you can mail merge using Excel, which makes printing labels of addresses and other things a lot simpler. A similar technique may also be used to generate RSVP lists, directories, and other lists that include a lot of information about individuals.

6. **Just for Fun:** It doesn't have to always be work and no pleasure when it comes to Excel. You can make a variety of other interesting things with the spreadsheet tool.

	A	B	C	D	E	F
1	FIRST NAME	LAST NAME	ADDRESS	CITY	STATE	ZIP CODE
2	Oprah	Winfrey	123 Magnificent Mile Ave.	Chicago	IL	58922
3	Mister	Rodgers	8935 Beautiful Day Rd.	New York	NY	23935
4	Hulk	Hogan	9284 Hollywood Blvd.	Los Angeles	CA	39825

- **Historical logs:** If you desire to keep track of the different craft beers you've tried, the exercises you've accomplished, or something else completely, Excel can help you keep everything organized and tracked.

Workout Log

Stats

Average Duration (minutes)	Average Calories
35	402

Average Distance (miles/km)	Average Weight
2.75	131

Average Pace (per hour)
4.88

Workouts

DATE	ACTIVITY	DURATION (minutes)	DISTANCE (miles/km)	PACE (per hour)	CALORIES	WEIGHT	
8/18/17	Cross Trainer	40	2.50	3.75	380	132	[Notes]
8/20/17	Treadmill	30	3.00	6.00	423	130	[Notes]

- **Sudoku puzzles:** Do you like Sudoku puzzles? You can create your own in Excel, Alternatively, if you're stuck on an especially tricky one, you may call the aid of MS Excel to help you figure it out!

X14

	A	B	C	D	E	F	G	H	I	J
1					1	7				
2	4						5			
3			9							
4						1		9		
5			5	7	8					
6	1			2					6	
7	5		4		2				3	
8	2				3	8		6	4	
9		1	3			9		5		

- **Word Cloud:** Word clouds aren't the most scientific way to portray facts. They are, however, a fascinating (not to mention gorgeous) method to learn about the most often used terms. Excel can be used to make one. You can make one in Wordle using MS excel.

- **Animations and Art:** Excel's capabilities are going to go well beyond what you may expect. Many individuals have utilized the program to make some very amazing artwork, ranging from animations to pixelated portraits.

- **Trip planner:** Do you have a trip planned? Before you make your bags and take all the necessary things with you and go, make sure that you have it all covered by making a handy itinerary. You can even use Excel to create a trip planning template to ensure you don't forget any of it (from your budgets to flight details!).

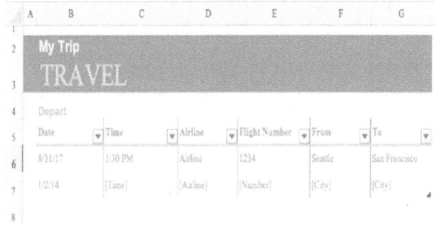

7. MS EXCEL USE In The Teaching And Learning Process

Microsoft Excel has become an indispensable tool in today's corporate world. It's even valuable in the academic realm, where it's used in a variety of creative ways. Let's look at how to properly utilize MS-Excel in the teaching and learning process.

- Teachers may turn any worksheet into a web page and can share it with students using Excel. This is a good technique to improve the efficiency of your teaching.

- Excel may help you learn visually. Teachers may create a visual demonstration of any content using this tool. Students will recall the lecture more easily with such a visual portrayal of the subject.

- MS-Excel is an excellent tool for instructors and academic professionals to use when analyzing any student or academic data. Excel macro apps may help you with a variety of tasks.

- Excel is also very beneficial for students. They utilize the software to create graphs and charts. It is becoming more important to the students for projects and other purposes.

- Excel may be used to create a comparison study of different school and student data.

8. **Uses of Excel for Housewives:** Excel may be used by housewives to keep track of their everyday household spending. They have the ability to generate monthly spending reports. They can keep track of their expenditure. Also, if women learn Excel, they would be able to teach basic Excel abilities to their children. It's because many computer instructors are unable to teach all Excel abilities to children in schools (for a variety of reasons). Excel may also be useful for housewives who are running a company or searching for part-time jobs. They can study and use excel to accomplish a variety of online and offline tasks and projects from home.

9. **Uses of MS Excel in Development of Your Career:** When you train yourself to succeed, you are also learning how to manage your everyday life. There are several things that must be considered in everyday living. What is the reason behind this? Because we have

various tasks to do on a daily basis. Shopping, studying, entertainment, and expenditures are all minor concerns that must be addressed. If you're a student, you should master Microsoft Excel as soon as possible. Knowing how to use Microsoft Excel can help you get a job. Because, as it is previously said, practically all small as well as medium firms, utilize Excel in their day-to-day operations. If you're writing about computer abilities on your resume, be sure you know how to use Excel and Microsoft Office, as well as how to do Internet research.

Career development is mostly about professional management than it is about career development. Goal-oriented habits, time management, work and life management, learning management are all critical. You may learn such stuff in Excel. When you produce your college expenditure report, you'll be able to see where you're spending more money at the end of each month. You may also use Excel to monitor knowledge if you're studying or taking online courses. Create a table containing Topic, Date, and Satisfaction Level if you learned about Conditional formatting today. This is advantageous since you will be able to comprehend your everyday learning results as well as the impacts of learning on you. For example, if you're studying digital marketing but aren't keeping track of your progress and making notes in 1 line conclusions, it'll be difficult to apply what you've learned afterward. For example, if you learned about CTR and PPC today, it's critical that you write about it in your journal or in Excel as a conclusion or summary.

This kind of learning and education management is critical. Because it often occurs when you learn anything on the web or via blogs, you often forget the major aspects as a result of alternative conclusions. For example, if someone tells you today to learn English typing, it's merely advice or a suggestion; but, if someone advises you to study English typing by utilizing fundamental typing classes like ASDF, LKJ, and others, it's critical that you write it down and practice it.

Some Points to Always Remember

There are a few things you should know about MS Excel, its apps, and how to use it:

- A .xls extension is used to save a Microsoft Excel file.

- MS Excel is used by companies with a big workforce and employees since it makes storing employee information simpler.

- The spreadsheet which you work on is termed a Worksheet

- A number of worksheets can be inserted into one single MS Excel file

- This is an information processing application

- Spreadsheets in excel can also be used in hospitals and health facilities where patient information can be stored more easily and removed easily once their medical records are cleared

Chapter 3: Microsoft Excel 2021

Microsoft's productivity software took a new path with the launching of Office 365 in 2011. Word, PowerPoint, and Excel had become accessible as components of the subscription service for the first time. The frequent upgrades were a key selling point since Office programs were only updated once every several years previously.

Office 365 was declared the most popular corporate cloud service less than 5 years after its introduction. It has now been renamed Microsoft 365, but the basic service that many users have grown to depend on remains the same. This includes One Drive, Outlook, and Microsoft Teams, which are included with business-focused subscriptions. Despite its popularity, Microsoft continues to offer separate versions of all of its strong Office applications every few years. These are simply referred to as 'Office' accompanied by the year of its release, with a 2021 version just announced recently. All you wish to know about the different versions of MS excel is right here.

3.1 Brief Review of Previous Versions of Excel

In 1985, the spreadsheet application was released solely for Macintosh, with a Microsoft version coming in 1987. Excel has gone through a lot of changes over the years to become the sophisticated spreadsheet program that we have today and love. A brief introduction about versions of MS excel except for the latest one (which we will discuss late in this chapter) below summarizes all of the many aspects of different versions of Excel, beginning with the first version in 1985 and ending with the most recent version in 2021. So here we are, with the release of the many versions of Microsoft Excel for Windows, which you may come across.

- **Version 1:** Released in 1985. This version of Excel was initially offered solely for Macintosh computers. Many Excel users are unaware of this, and it may seem weird. Microsoft had previously attempted to produce a spreadsheet application called Multiplan in 1982, but it was unsuccessful. Until 2016, Excel versions for various operating systems were known by distinct names.

- **Excel 2:** Released in 1987. To correlate to the Mac version, the initial MS Excel edition for Windows was designated "2." It was a port of the Mac "Excel 2" and contained a run-time version for Windows.

- **Excel 3:** Released in 1990. Toolbars, outlining, drawing capabilities, 3D charts, add-in support, and many more additional innovations and features were included in this next edition.

- **Excel 4:** Released in 1992. Version 4 was the first "famous" version of Excel. Many usability enhancements were implemented, including AutoFill, which was originally offered in this version.

- **Excel 5:** Released in 1993. Excel 5 was a significant update. It had multi-worksheet workbooks as well as Macros AND VBA support. Excel became more susceptible to macro virus assaults as a result of these new features, which REMAINED to be a concern until the 2007 edition.

- **Excel 95**: Released in 1995. It was the first main 32-bit version of Excel, and it was known as Excel 95. Excel 5 featured a 32-bit version as well, although it was not extensively utilized owing to distribution issues. Excel 95 is pretty comparable to Excel 5 in terms of features. You might also be asking why Excel 6 isn't available. Beginning with Excel 7, all MS Office apps have been using the same version number, so the version numbering has been modified.

- **Excel 97**: Released in 1997. This version included a new VBA developer interface, data validation, User Forms, and much more. Do you remember Clippy, the obnoxious Office Assistant? He was also a member of this version.

- **Excel 2000:** Released in 1999. HTML as a local file format, a "self-repair" capability, an upgraded clipboard, modeless user forms and pivot charts are among the new features.

- **Excel 2002**: Released in 2001. This was the first time Excel was included in Office XP. The vast list of new features didn't contribute much to the ordinary user's experience. The new capability that enabled you to restore your work if Excel crashes were among the most important innovations. This version also had a helpful feature called product activation technology (commonly called copy protection), which limits the usage of the program to one computer at a time. Before determining whether or not to update, you had to think about the consequences.

- **Microsoft Office Excel 2003**: Released in 2003. Improved XML support, a new "list range" tool, Smart Tag upgrades, and updated statistical functions were among the new features in this version. The majority of consumers did not consider the data upgrade beneficial.

- **Microsoft Office Excel 2007**: Released in 2007. Excel underwent significant modifications in this Windows edition. The Ribbon interface was introduced, as well as a change in the file format type from .xls to the now-familiar .xlsx and .xlsm. This modification improved Excel's security (referred to the difficulties with macro viruses in previous versions) and allowed for additional row data storage (over one million). The charting features have also been considerably enhanced. To the delight of some and the dismay of others, Clippy was removed from Microsoft Excel as part of the upgrade.

- **Microsoft Office Excel 2010**: Released in 2010. Sparkline graphics, an updated Solver, pivot table slicers, and a 64-bit version were among the new additional features in this MS Excel version.

- **Microsoft Excel 2013**: Released in 2013. Over 50 new functions were included in this edition, as well as a single-document interface suggested pivot tables and charts and additional charting improvements.

- **Microsoft Excel 2016**: Released in 2016. Despite the fact that they were separate versions of the program, Excel for Windows and Mac was known as the same thing after this version came out. If you had a subscription to Office 365, you get unique Excel Internet updates that may drastically improve your user experience. Older versions and those purchased from a store are consequently at a disadvantage. Histograms (to illustrate the frequency in data), Power Pivot (which allowed for the input of greater levels of data and included its own language), and Pareto charts (to display data trends) were some of the new features in this edition.

- **Microsoft Excel 2019**: Released in 2019. This version had all of the capabilities found in previous versions of Excel, as well as some new ones. The new charts, which provide a unique twist to data presentation, are one of the most noticeable new additions. Funnel charts and Map charts are two examples of modern data presentation charts that make your data seem tidy; they both were added in this version. In addition, the option of using 3D images in your workbooks was introduced.

If you have an older version of MS Excel, it will probably work with newer files if you use the compatibility mode. Keep in mind that previous versions have many fewer features that are understandable if you've been paying attention to the changing features in the previous versions. Some of them may not be functional with the newer operating systems, but it's a good idea to try out several versions and look at how the same file appears in each.

3.2 All about MS Excel 2021

Microsoft Excel 2021 will have an improved interface, new tools that will enable users to manage data in Microsoft Excel more flexibly, and other enhancements, according to Microsoft. In Excel 2021, two brand new features will be included. The first, known as dynamic arrays, will add to Excel's data-analytics property. The spreadsheet editor comes with a huge number of pre-made formulas that may be used to do things like calculating the average quarterly income for the last two years. In most cases, a formula's output is condensed into one spreadsheet cell, which might cause formatting challenges for advanced business calculations with several outputs. To save time, dynamic arrays arrange findings into different cells automatically.

Excel will also get a feature called XLOOKUP from Microsoft, which allows users to look for data in a particular spreadsheet row rather than wading through the whole spreadsheet. This is especially beneficial in complicated documents with a big number of identical components. A user may, for example, find the row having the name of a vehicle component and then utilize the XLOOKUP option to rapidly move to the cell in that same row showing the component's price.

3.3 Detailed Feature Updates

Excel has made its users happy and contended by introducing all the latest and most useful tools and features in its software. In the upcoming latest version of Excel 2021, there are some significant feature updates that people who frequently use excel would love to read about. If you want to know about all the new features, then keep going further in this chapter. All the feature updates that will be included in the brand new version of Excel is Excel 2021, are discussed below.

1. **Automatically Use New Data Types:** Excel suggests converting a data value that matches a geographic location or a stock to the appropriate associated data type of Stocks or Geography when you input it.

Excel Data Types:

- **Stocks and Geography:** Excel may be used to get geographic and stock data. It's as simple as typing any text into a cell then turning it into the Geography data or Stocks data type. As they have a link to an online web data source, these 2 data types are termed linked data types. This link enables you to get rich, intriguing data that you may work with and update.

Note: If Excel recognizes what you're typing as a geographic location or tradable financial instrument, it will suggest a linked data type for you to use (Stocks or Geography). Only Microsoft 365 customers or those having a free Microsoft Account may access the Geography or Stocks data types.

- **Linked data types:** It provides you with real-world facts. New linked data types in Excel deliver you data and facts on hundreds of topics to help you achieve your objectives.

- **Creating Data Types:** You may use the Advanced Dialog to manually pick the columns that make up the Data Type you're making.

2. **Unhide Many Sheets at the Same Time:** It's no longer necessary to unhide a single sheet at a time; instead, you may unhide numerous concealed sheets at the same time. To make a worksheet invisible, you may hide it. Although the data in hidden worksheets is hidden, it may still be accessed from other workbooks or worksheets, and hidden worksheets can be readily unhidden as required. To un-hide sheets, right-click any visible sheet or the sheet tab you wish to hide. Choose one of the following options from the menu that appears:

- Select Hide to conceal the sheet.

- To reveal hidden sheets, pick them in Unhide dialogue box that opens, then click OK.

- To choose numerous sheets, perform one of the following:

- Hold CTRL while clicking the items to choose them.

- Press and then hold SHIFT, then change your selection using the up or down arrow keys.

3. **Integrated Stock Prices:** With their new Data Types capability, Microsoft stated that Excel users would be able to extract real-time stock price data right into their spreadsheet cells. When predicting anything, particularly stocks, having access to previous data is essential. We can design (and share) our own algorithms that automatically examine thousands of stocks and indicate those we may wish to invest in using this data accessible to Excel users. Users will also be able to create their very own strategies for portfolio and back-test them to determine whether they are practical to implement. Although such data is currently accessible via third parties, obtaining it for free and without needing to input files on a regular basis would be a significant victory for personal financial enthusiasts.

Stock Name	52 Wk Low	52 Wk High	Price	% Change
🏛 Microsoft Corp (XNAS:MSFT)	$93.96	$158.67	$158.67	+0.82%
🏛 Alphabet Inc (XNAS:GOOG)	$983.00	$1,365.00	$1,360.40	+1.25%
🏛 Verizon Communications Inc (XNYS:VZ)	$52.28	$62.22	$61.29	+0.02%
🏛 Walt Disney Co (XNYS:DIS)	$100.38	$153.41	$145.70	+0.28%
🏛 Apple Inc (XNAS:AAPL)	$142.00	$289.91	$289.91	+1.98%
🏛 Facebook Inc (XNAS:FB)	$125.89	$208.66	$207.79	+1.30%

4. Automate Data Analysis with Excel's Ideas Feature: Ideas is an artificial intelligence feature in Excel 2021 that is accessible with Office 365 subscriptions. Excel can swiftly evaluate your data with Ideas and give you insights you may not have spotted otherwise. The 'Ideas' function is Microsoft's most daring effort into the use of artificial intelligence and machine learning in Excel. At its most basic level, Excel allows you to highlight a piece of data and have it analyzed, with proposed visualizations (charts) and comments to help you understand it. It's a fascinating concept, and the concept that the systems are always improving depending on the data sent to them and how the customers utilize the 'ideas' is something to be excited about. Now, I don't think this technology will ever replace financial analysts (there's a reason it's named "Ideas" rather than "Answers"), but you should see it as a way to get a second opinion on our data or to automate the analysis-creation process. It will be fascinating to

observe how this technology evolves in the next years, as well as how often Excel users will utilize it.

- Ideas might be beneficial in the following scenarios, for example:

- Rank data and find objects that are considerably smaller or bigger as compared to the rest of the population by analyzing transactions;

- Using trend analysis to identify patterns in data that have developed over time;

- Identifying major anomalies in data points, such as fraudulent transactions or possibly erroneous

- Drawing attention to instances where a single element accounts for a major amount of the entire value.

- You may access the 'Ideas' from the main Home tab of the Ribbon if you have an Office 365 subscription. However, in order to utilize this functionality, you should have an internet connection.

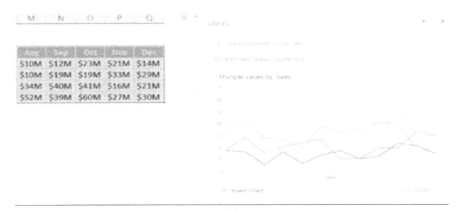

5. **Simpler Conditional Formulas with IFS, MAXIFS, and MINIFS:** You can write formulas that include numerous tests more easily than before using IFS, MAXIFS, and MINIFS. Many Excel users used to "nest" many 'IF' functions in the same calculation before IFS became available. When you needed to do a computation based on one or more circumstances, this was a frequent approach. However, with the development of IFS, such formulations have been substantially simplified. For example, observe how just a single IFS function is needed in the formula written below to run three tests on the data in cell A2. This method avoids the need for several IF functions, which would have been necessary previously. MAXIFS and MINIFS, like IFS, allow you to run many tests on your data. When utilizing MAXIFS, when all of the tests are passed, Excel will give the highest value. When utilizing MINIFS, on the other hand, when all of the conditions are passed, Excel returns the lowest number. Excel 2021 users will have access to these capabilities. They're also accessible to Office 365 subscribers who have access to Excel.

6. **XLOOKUP – A Better and Easier Alternative to VLOOKUP:** Beginning in February 2020, Microsoft will bring XLOOKUP to Excel as part of Office 365. VLOOKUP and comparable functions like HLOOKUP

and INDEX are pale in comparison to XLOOKUP. While Excel will retain these older functionalities, many people are going to discover XLOOKUP to be much more easy and intuitive. Most people will discover that XLOOKUP is significantly more powerful.

The following are some of the key distinctions between other lookup functions and XLOOKUP:

- XLOOKUP uses an exact match by default, while VLOOKUP and HLOOKUP use an approximate match.

- Unlike VLOOKUP and HLOOKUP, you do not need to provide a row index number or a column index number with XLOOKUP.

- With XLOOKUP, the order of rows and columns is unimportant. This is because, when used as a replacement for VLOOKUP, it can look left or right. When used as a replacement for HLOOKUP, it can also look above or below.

- XLOOKUP eliminates the need for an IFERROR function by allowing you to describe what happened if your search value isn't found.

- VLOOKUP, IFERROR, HLOOKUP and INDEX/MATCH are all combined into one simplified Excel function with XLOOKUP. This is the feature that you will all be teaching your children how to use before their first job interview, and it is one that you will assure to use on a regular basis within the corporate sector.

H3						fx	=XLOOKUP(H2,B3:B15,D3:D15,"Item Not Found")	
	A	B	C	D	E	F	G	H
1								
2		Item	Description	Unit Price	QOH		Part Number	C003
3		C001	Creme, Aloe Vera Hand, 9 oz	6.99	143		Unit Price	12.99
4		C002	Creme, Extra Moisturizing Hand, 9 oz	7.49	109		Quantity On Hand	72
5		C003	Creme, Hand and Body, 16 oz	12.99	72			
6		L001	Lotion, Organic Body, 9 oz	7.99	68			
7		L002	Lotion, Organic Body, 16 oz	14.99	148			
8		L003	Lotion, Organic Body, 24 oz.	21.99	106			
9		L201	Lotion, Extra Moisturizing Body, 9 oz	6.99	165			
10		L202	Lotion, Organic Hand and Body, 9 oz	8.49	138			
11		L203	Lotion, Organic Hand and Body, 16 oz	15.99	63			
12		M101	Mask, Organic Facial, 9 oz	13.99	89			
13		M102	Mask, Wrinkle Reducing Facial, 9 oz	18.99	34			
14		M201	Mask, Wrinkle Reducing Facial, 16 oz	35.99	58			
15		M202	Mask, Wrinkle Reducing Facial, 24 oz	53.99	69			

7. **Dynamic Arrays:** Another new feature update that is now only accessible with a subscription to Office 365 is dynamic arrays. You can use dynamic arrays to create one single formula that affects numerous cells at the same time without having to replicate the formula to all of them. You also don't need to utilize the CTRL + SHIFT + ENTER keyboard sequence to enter a typical array formula if you're using an Excel version that supports dynamic arrays. Furthermore, if you're using an Excel

version that has dynamic arrays function, you'll have access to six additional functions to help you take use of this newfound ability. FILTER, RANDARRY, SORT, SEQUENCE, UNIQUE and SORTBY are the six functions.

Illustrating Dynamic Arrays: Let's see how to use the new FILTER function to provide a basic example of dynamic arrays. The FILTER function, as its name suggests, may be used to filter data in a range or table using a formula. The syntax is straightforward, as demonstrated below.

=FILTER (array (range or table), include (a Boolean array for which items to include))

The basic FILTER example presented should demonstrate the value of dynamic arrays: they let you evaluate data using formulas, and the formula outputs are related to the raw data set but do not disrupt it. As a result, instead of copying the data numerous times, you may do several sorts of analyses on the very same underlying data set. Do you recall wanting to create a complicated formula, looking for it on the web, and then copying and pasting it into your worksheet with the instructions to type ctrl+shift+enter after that? Who wonders why you had to do that, but it worked like a charm! That formula you came upon was the formula of an Array. Curly brackets around these formulas (auto-inserted with ctrl+shift+enter) were required to notify Excel what to assume since they produce various responses.

Microsoft unveiled a new set of functions in early 2019 that has radically changed the way we create complicated calculations as users. These new Dynamic Array functions have reduced the complex/lengthy formulas of the past into easy, dynamic functions that everyone can use.....and the greatest thing is that you no longer need to utilize the ctrl+shift+enter keyboard sequence! UNIQUE was one of the initial capabilities included in Microsoft's initial suite. Simply give unique a range of cells, and it will return each and every one of the unique values it discovers in individual cells (eliminating duplicate values). Even further, if your set of values expands or contracts over time, the list provided by the UNIQUE formula will update accordingly.

H3				▾	:	×	✓	f_x	=UNIQUE($D$4:$D$11)	
	A	B	C	D	E	F	G		H	
1										
2										
3				State				Unique States:	Ohio	
4				Ohio					California	
5				California					New York	
6				New York					New Mexico	
7				Ohio					Florida	
8				Ohio						
9				New Mexico						
10				Florida						
11				Florida						
12										

8. Analyze the Quality of Your Data with Power Query:

Power Query: Power Query is a data cleansing automation tool that is now immediately included in Excel's Get & Transform Data group on the Data tab. You can link to tables or data sources inside Excel files and then construct clean-up rules with a single push of a button. You may opt to create these rules and generate them using menus/forms in the order you want them to happen. Splitting first and last names into distinct columns, conducting calculations, eliminating blank rows, etc., are just a few examples. Once you've generated all of your rules, you may save them and repeat them anytime you like. The progress of Power Query, which debuted with Excel 2010's release, has been nothing short of astounding. You may use this tool to import data into Excel from a variety of external sources of data, including the databases that support the majority of accounting software. More significantly, you can utilize Power Query to modify your data such that it becomes more helpful to you. These changes might involve, among other things, removing unnecessary data columns, combining columns, filtering and sorting, and adding user-defined calculations as part of the query. Power Query's ability to automatically examine your data for quality concerns like completeness and correctness is a recent development. You can immediately identify possible issue areas using this functionality, such as incorrect data, missing entries, and even duplicated entries. Check the Column distribution, Column quality, and Column profile boxes on the Power Query Editor's view tab to make use of this feature. Moreover, clicking on any specific column in the query displays a more thorough view of data, which includes a value distribution graph and statistics for that specific column. Microsoft seems to go all-in about what they term its "Power" programs in the latter half of the last decade. These are mostly cloud-based programs that can simply import data from other sources (such as databases or webpages) and run automated procedures to produce a clean final product. Take survey findings, combine them with data of sales, and compile them into a monthly display that your Sales VPs may access on their mobile devices. These Power Applications are all about the capacity to channel in all kinds of data from apps and automate the joining and cleansing and of that data. This is certainly a talent that organizations will be searching for in the coming years, and Excel users can hop right in and acquire quite quickly with a little effort. Power Query, as well as Power BI, are the 2 major functions of excel that you should be focusing on. There's a lot of demand for people with these skill sets right now.

Power BI: Power BI (Business Intelligence) is a specialized dashboard-building tool. It makes it simple to link to third-party sources of data like Google Analytics, Salesforce, and social media to get real-time data. From there, you can use a variety of dashboard modules (such as slicers and charts) to create any kind of final dashboard you can imagine. After that, you can simply share your newly generated dashboard with your whole organization, with all of your information security settings in place (if anyone only has access to a single subset of the database and they can only view that subset present in the dashboard).

9. The Dark Mode Addition which make Things Simpler

Dark mode users claim that it improves the clarity between the text you're reading and the surrounding environment. This should potentially make computer reading simpler. Medium grey and Black are the default themes of Microsoft Office. By choosing a dark theme, you may alter the look of Office products like Microsoft Word, Excel, PowerPoint and Outlook. The dark option would be much better, making everything considerably darker and easier on the eyes. The dark backdrop may make late-night editing and writing much easier. Microsoft Word's dark option currently just darkens the document's borders, leaving the remainder bright white. You will be capable to darken the whole paper in a future release.

3.4 Overall Benefits of Using MS Excel 2021

MS Excel is extensively used for a variety of reasons, including the ease with which data can be information can be inserted and withdrawn and saved with no effort. A few fundamental and essential advantages of using Microsoft Excel 2021 are listed below:

- **Easy To Recover Data:** Finding information written on a paper might take longer, but that isn't the situation with excel spreadsheets. It's simple to locate and retrieve data.

- **Mathematical Formulas application:** With the formulas feature in MS Excel, doing mathematical calculations has become simpler and less time-consuming.

- **Easy To Save Data:** MS Excel is extensively used to save and analyses data since there is no restriction to the quantity of data that can be recorded in a spreadsheet. Filtering data in Excel is simple and straightforward.

- **More Secure:** These spreadsheets are password protected on a laptop or desktop computer, and the risk of losing them is far lower than data stored in registers or on paper.

- **Clearer** and **Neater and Visibility of data:** Analyzing data gets simpler when it is recorded in tabular form. As a result, information is more understandable and readable in a spreadsheet.

- **All Data at One Place:** When the documentation was completed, data was previously held in various files and registers. More than one worksheet may now be added to a single MS Excel file, making this more practical.

Excel allows users to analyze, organize, and evaluate quantitative results, enabling senior staff and managers to make key choices that might affect the firm with the knowledge they need. Employees that are taught in advanced Excel functions will be able to present their data more effectively to senior management. It's also a necessary talent for individuals who want to work their way to the top. Employers and Employees can benefit from superior Excel knowledge. Let's take a closer look at the benefits of Excel when it is a part of the company's regular staff training.

3.5 Advantages of Excel 2021 for Employees

Advanced Excel training may help your employees in a variety of ways, from improving their value to learning new tools to boost their job performance.

Sharpening Your Skill Set: To progress in your profession, you must continue to study and polish your skills. Appropriate training of Excel focuses on a variety of important abilities that may be used and appreciated in practically every job role. You should be able to:

- Visualize, modify, and analyses data after training.

- Develop equations that will enable you to deliver additional information on critical corporate activities, including workflow, financial estimates, project efficiency, and inventory levels and utilization as well as budgets,

- Create an easy-to-understand data collection that higher management may utilize to assess current initiatives or conditions in the firm.

- Create spreadsheets that better organize data and provide a clearer view of what's being entered.

- Read and understand data and spreadsheets from other departments, suppliers, and customers.

- The ability to evaluate data at a higher level allows you to provide solutions to business challenges.

- Organize, balance, and maintain complicated inventory and financial accounts.

- Set up tracking systems for various departments and activities, as well as distinct workflow processes.

- Comprehensive MS Excel training will supply organizations with higher-skilled personnel as well as tools to assist workers in operating more efficiently in their existing roles and preparing them for advancement to higher-level roles.

Improving Your Productivity and Efficiency: When dealing with big volumes of data and computations, Excel is a critical tool for increasing productivity and helping employees to be more efficient. When you have a deeper understanding of Excel, you will be able to utilize its more complex capabilities, which will help you to finish jobs and analyses data more rapidly. It will also enable you to keep your team members informed about data, which will help to speed up the workflow process. Even better, mastering advanced Excel can help you improve the efficiency of your computations. Calculations that have to be repeated take time, particularly when you have to check your work twice. You may make more complex computations using advanced Excel features. Once you've typed your formula and entered your set instructions, the software will do the calculations for you, saving up a lot of time for other chores and guaranteeing that you get correct results the first time.

Making Yourself a More Valuable Member of the Company: Being a valued employee not only ensures your job stability but also allows you to grow your career. Being more efficient, more educated, and knowledgeable in your work tasks can help you become more valuable to the firm. That is what advanced Excel training can deliver. To prevent being replaced by fresher employees with a more developed skillset, employees should continuously look for methods to boost their benefits to the company. To put yourself up for better security and development, you must learn and master new skills.

Making You Better at Organizing Data: Spreadsheets are a popular tool for gathering and organizing data. MS Excel is in its most basic form. It enables you to meticulously arrange all of the data while also allowing you to arrange the information in whatever manner you like. Data in its raw form may be overwhelming and difficult to understand. With Excel's amazing features, you'll be able to better organize your data, do computations as needed, and sort the data so that it can be properly examined and transferred to charts or graphs for easier viewing.

It Can Make Your Job Easier: The more familiar you are with Excel, the faster you will be able to manage the system. Microsoft Excel has a number of shortcuts that may help you work quicker and even discover more complex Excel tactics that you may use throughout the full Microsoft Office suite. You'll also be able to utilize the information in your Excel spreadsheet in a number of tools, decreasing the need to re-enter data and improving the efficiency of your workflow. The simpler your job is to do, the more prepared you are to do it and more probably you are to love it.

3.6 Advantages of Advanced Excel for Employers

Advanced Excel knowledge and expertise may bring several advantages for both your staff and your company.

- It boosts your company's productivity by increasing efficiency.

- It enables you to make better use of the assets you've already acquired, such as software applications.

- It enables you to increase employee understanding with little cost and effort.

- It relieves your IT support team of stress, allowing them to concentrate on more productive activities like system updates, security maintenance, and hardware installation and maintenance.

Chapter 4: Creating Workbook Using MS Excel 2021

Excel makes number crunching simple. With AutoFill in Excel, you can speed up data entering. Then, depending on your data, receive chart suggestions and generate them with a single click. With data bars, icons, and color-coding, you can immediately discover trends and patterns.

After you've mastered Excel's fundamental menus and capabilities, it's time to fill up a spreadsheet with data and observe how Excel handles it. When you hear the word "spreadsheet" in relation to Excel, you most often imagine an Excel file. Microsoft, on the other hand, distinguishes between workbooks and worksheets. You'll have to know the distinction between the two characteristics as you deal with several Excel files.

4.1 Worksheets vs. Workbooks

It may seem like a minor distinction, but knowing the differences between a workbook and a worksheet in Excel is critical when dealing with formulas and connected files. A new workbook is created when you a new Excel file. An Excel file is referred to as a workbook.

Excel automatically adds a new sheet once you create a workbook. The name of that sheet may be seen in the bottom-left corner of the current workbook window. The worksheet's default name is "Sheet1," that you can see in the lower right corner. Within a single workbook, Excel enables you to create many worksheets. Each page in the workbook may be used to hold data categorized by type. Each sheet may relate to other sheets in the workbook. For example, a workbook called "Customer Orders" may include two pages. Customer shipping information is on one page, while order information is on the other. To identify the address to distribute the product, a worksheet having customer orders might relate to the worksheet having customer shipping data. Keep an eye out for the "+" symbol next to the already opened sheet at the bottom of the workbook window. When you click it, a new sheet with the next number is produced. "Sheet1" is the default name for the first sheet. The following sheet name is "Sheet2" when you add a new sheet. Even if you use the default names for your worksheets, each worksheet in the workbook must have its own name.

4.2 Create a Workbook

A workbook is a document that includes one or many more worksheets to aid with data organization. A template or an empty workbook or may be used to start a new workbook. In Excel, you may quickly create a new workbook. The workbook is in the default file type, similar to how in Word. Multiple worksheets may be found in a workbook, where information is processed and stored in columns and rows.

A startup screen shows when you first launch Excel. From the template list on the right of the screen, you may make a new workbook from this launch page. If you already have a worksheet open, the "File" tab on the Ribbon will take you to a similar screen. Then, on the left of the backstage view, pick the "New" command. Then, on the right of the backstage view, a list of templates emerges. Then, by picking the selected template, you may create a brand new workbook from any of the many accessible templates. In Excel, choose the template option of "Blank workbook" in the right-hand corner to start a new blank workbook. Entering Data in a Worksheet: After you've set up your worksheet, you can start filling in the cells. Excel provides a variety of formatting options for inputting data and dealing with alphanumeric values rather than numbers and computations.

- Start Excel.

- Press Ctrl+N or choose Blank workbook.

- Begin typing.

- Input data

- Select an unfilled cell, like A1, and input number or text to manually input data.

- To proceed to the next cell, press Enter or Tab.

- To complete a sequence of data:

- In two cells, write the start of the series, such as January and February, or any other.

- Move the fill slider down or across the cells to choose the two cells that contain the series.

The Three Types of Data: Text, formula and value are the three forms of data. This is the kind of information you put into cells. If Excel recognizes the item as a formula, the formula will be calculated, and the result will be shown in the cell. When the cell is active, you can view the formula in the Formula Bar. If Excel discovers that it isn't a formula, it determines if it is text or value. The entries of 'text' are placed on the cell's left side. On the Right-hand side, 'values' are aligned. This information is necessary so that you can ensure that you are entering data properly and that Excel recognizes your input as the right data type.

1. **Text Data type:** Text entries are just pieces of information that Excel can't recognize as a formula or a value. The majority of the text items are labeled. Column and row labels are the titles of the columns and rows. If Excel is identifying your data as text, the text will always be positioned to the cell's left side.

2. **Values:** Values are the fundamental components of any formulas your input. Values are the numbers that represent amounts as well as dates. The cell's values are positioned to the right side. Excel will assume that the

values you provide as formula are values if it can't solve them.

Adding Values: Now, let us see how you can enter values in the MS Excel worksheet.

- **Negative values**. If you want to insert a negative value, precede it with a minus (-) symbol. If you wish, you can also use parentheses. If you use parentheses, Excel will transform it to a negative value.

- **Dollar amounts**. You can add commas and dollar signs if you are writing a value that is a dollar amount, exactly as you would if you were putting it by hand.

- **Decimal points**. You can use the period key if you wish to put a decimal point on your keyboard.

- **Fractions**. There's no need to panic if you need to transform a fraction to a decimal since Excel can do it for you. Simply use the slash key present on the keyboard to enter the fraction. Before entering the fraction, be sure to leave a gap after any whole numbers.

3. **Formulas:** A formula in Excel is just an expression that conducts a calculation. It might be as easy as 5 + 2 or more complicated. You can do calculations in a single cell and in a range of cells, depending upon the elements in 2 different cells, or also in a range of cells over many spreadsheets. A chosen group or block of cells is referred

to as a range of cells. Don't worry if this is all a little unclear right now. It will be crystal clear when you will further go through this chapter. For the time being, remember that every calculation you put into Excel must begin with an equals to sign (=). This may seem unusual at first since an equals sign normally appears at the conclusion of an expression, but it informs Excel that you wish to do a calculation right away. So you always begin with an equals to sign in Excel when you wish to add a formula.

Create a workbook from a template: If you don't want to create a blank workbook at the beginning, you can also start your workbook with a number of templates that Excel offers to their users, and it is very simple to use a template. To start with it,

- Click on File and then on the New option.

- A number of templates would appear on your window.

- Click twice on a template that you want to start with.

- After Clicking, that template would be open and just start typing.

4.3 Save Your Workbook to One-Drive in Excel

Save a worksheet to One-Drive so that you may access it from several devices and interact with others.

- Choose File and then Save As from the File menu.

- Choose whether you want it for school or work.

- Choose a name for One-Drive, and for Personal files, select One-drive personal.

- Choose Save after entering a file name.

- It's possible that you'll need to log in to your MS account.

4.4 Add or Remove a Worksheet

In Microsoft Excel it is very easy to add, delete and rename spreadsheets in your workbook file.

Add a worksheet:

- Choose the sum icon which means add (+) below on the screen displayed.

Or,

- You can click on the Home tab, then go on Insert and then choose the option of Add Sheet.

Renaming the worksheet:

- Click twice on the name of the sheet and easily change the name.

Or,

- You can click on the tab labeled as Sheet with the right-click and then go to Rename option and write a new one.

Remove a worksheet:

- You can right-click on the Sheet tab and then select Delete.

Or,

- Choose the sheet, and then go to the Home tab and select the Delete option and click on Delete Sheet.

4.5 Change the location or Copy Worksheets or Worksheet Data

To arrange your workbook precisely as you want it, you can change the place of your worksheet or duplicate worksheets within the same workbook. To transfer or copy whole worksheets to other places in the same or other workbooks, just use the Move or Copy Sheet function. Use the Cut and Copy commands. To relocate or transfer a section of the data to another worksheet or workbook

Move a worksheet within a workbook: Choose the worksheet tab and drag it to the desired location. Before transferring a sheet to some other workbook, double-check any formulas or charts that relate to data on the sheet since changing the sheet might result in data mistakes or undesired effects. Similarly, if you shift a sheet with 3-D references, the algorithm may include or exclude data from the sheet.

Copy a worksheet in the same workbook

- Hold CTRL and slide the tab of the worksheet to the desired spot.

Or,

- Right-click on the worksheet tab and choose Move or Copy.

- Choose and make a copy checkbox.

- Below the before sheet, choose where you want the copy to go.

- Click OK.

4.6 Analyze and Format In Excel

Automatically fill the column with Flash Fill: Fill the First Name column with data from a Full Name column, for example.

- Type Molly in the field under the First Name and hit Enter.

- Type the first several letters of Garret in the following cell.

- Press Return when the range of recommended values shows.

- To see additional possibilities, go to Flash Fill Options.

Quickly calculate with AutoSum:

- Go to the cell underneath the numbers you wish to add and select it.

- Choose the Home tab and then AutoSum from the drop-down menu.

- Hit the Enter key.

Tip: To add additional calculations, click the down arrow beside the AutoSum and choose one.

- In the status bar, you may also pick a range of values to display typical calculations.

Create a chart: Select the appropriate chart for your data using the Quick Analysis tool.

- Choose the information you wish to display in a chart.

- Go to the below and right of the chosen cells and click the Quick Analysis button.

- Choose Charts from the drop-down menu, then scroll over the selections to choose the chart you like.

Use conditional formatting: To highlight essential data or display data patterns, use Quick Analysis.

- Choose the data you want to format conditionally.

- Go to the below and right of the chosen cells and click the Quick Analysis button.

- Scroll over the choices under Formatting and choose the one you like.

Freeze the top row of headings: Only the data moves while the uppermost row of column heads is frozen.

- When you're finished modifying a cell, press Enter or Esc.

- Choose the View tab and then go to the Freeze Panes. Select the Freeze Top Row option from the View menu.

Create a drop-down list: Drop-down menus in cells may help individuals work more effectively in workbooks. People may choose an object from a list you build using drop-down menus. Type the items you wish to show in your drop-down menu list in a new spreadsheet. Your list elements should ideally be organized in an MS Excel table. If you don't, you may easily convert your prepared list into a table by using Ctrl+T on any of the cells in the range.

- In the worksheet, choose the cell where you'd like the drop-down list to appear.

- Select Data Validation from the Data tab on the Ribbon.

- Click List in the Allow box on the Settings tab.

- Select the listed range by clicking in the Source box.

- Checkmark the Ignore blank box if it's okay for users to leave the cell empty.

- Select In-cell from the dropdown box.

- Go to the tab of Input Message.

Note: Check the 'Show input message when a cell is the selected box and write a message and title in the boxes (almost 225 characters) if you desire a message to appear when the cell is clicked. Uncheck the check box if you don't need a message to appear.

- Go to the tab of Error Alert.

Note: To have a message appear when someone types anything that isn't on your list, select the Show error warning when invalid data is entered in the box, choose a style from the Style box, and create a title and message. Uncheck the check box if you don't like a message to appear.

- Click Warning or Information to display a notice that does not prevent individuals from putting data that isn't in the drop-down list.

- Click Stop to prevent users from putting data that isn't in the drop-down list.

Note: if you don't add a text or title, the title and message will default to "Microsoft Excel" and "The value you inserted is not acceptable. A user has limited values that may be input into this field."

- Make sure your drop-down list goes the way you want it to once you've finished creating it. Check to see whether you can change the row height and column width to display all of your entries.

- Consider concealing and safeguarding that worksheet if the list of items for your drop-down menu list is on any other worksheet and you don't want people to view it or make changes to it. Check Lock cells to secure them for further information on how to safeguard a worksheet.

- See 'Add or delete things from the drop-down list if you wish to update the choices in your drop-down menu.

- Visit 'Remove a drop-down list' for instructions if you want to delete your drop-down list.

4.7 Print a Workbook or Worksheet

You may easily print whole or partial workbooks and worksheets one by one or in batches. You can also print simply the Excel table if that data you wish to publish is in an MS Excel table. Instead of printing to a printer, you may save a workbook as a file. This is important if you wish to get a print of your workbook on a printer that isn't the same as that you were using before. When you print something in Excel, keep in mind that there are a variety of choices for getting the best print results.

Note: Certain formatting, like cell shading or colorful text, may seem fine on the computer but may not appear as expected when printed in white and black. You could also wish to get a print of the spreadsheet with gridlines to make the data, columns or rows stand out more clearly.

For Windows: You may print one or more worksheets.

- Choose which worksheets you wish to print.

- Select File and then Print from the menu bar or you can hit CTRL+P on your keyboard.

- Select the Print option right away or make any necessary adjustments to the settings before pressing the Print option.

Print One as well as Several Workbooks: You must keep your all Excel files in one folder if you wish to print them.

- Select File and then open from the File menu.

- Press CTRL and click the title of every single workbook you want to print, then press Print option.

Print a Part or a Complete Worksheet:

- Select the spreadsheet and then choose the set of data you like to print.

- Select File, then Print from the drop-down menu.

- Below Settings, Select the appropriate option, then drag the arrow beside Print All Active Sheets option.

- Select Print option.

Note: It is important to see If Sheet has print regions defined, Excel will only print those print regions.

Print table using MS Excel: To make the table active, tap a cell within it.

- Select File, then Print from the drop-down menu.

- Select 'Print Selected Table' from the arrow beside the Print All Active Sheets option in the Settings menu.

- Select Print option.

Print the Excel Workbook to the File:

- Press Ctrl+P, or select File, and print.

- Press 'Print to File' from the Printer menu.

- Select Print.

- Click OK after entering a file name in 'Save the Print Output' as a dialogue box. The file now will be stored in the Documents folder of your computer.

- The font spacing and page breaks may vary if you have printed the saved document on another printer.

For Web:

Get a Print of the Worksheet: Utilize the Print instruction in MS Excel for web rather than the Print command in your browser to print your worksheet for the best results. You have the option of printing the complete worksheet or only some cells that are needed to print. Select the cells you wish to print if you'd like to get a print of a group of cells. Don't choose anything if you want to print the complete worksheet.

- Select the File tab and then Print from the File menu.

- Before hitting Print, switch to Complete Workbook if you picked the desired cells and want to get a print of complete worksheet.

Transform the Selected Area of Print: You have the option of printing a specific section or the complete worksheet in MS Excel. If you choose a specific area for your print and later decide to modify it, here are the steps that you can use to see how your changes will look:

- Choose the number of cells you wish to print by clicking and dragging on the worksheet.

- Select the File tab and then Print from the File menu.

- Click 'Current Selection' in the displayed Options to print just the desired region.

- Click Print if the preview of the print displays what you wish to get printed.

- Close the preview of print by pressing the X, then repeat the same steps that you have followed earlier to modify the print choices.

- Select the File tab and then print the full worksheet. Ensure that the Complete Sheet is chosen and then click Print.

- You can choose additional print settings if you are having the MS Excel desktop program. Select numerous print regions on a spreadsheet by clicking Open in Excel.

Get a print of the Worksheet That Has Concealed Columns and Rows: When you get a print of spreadsheet with concealed columns or rows in Excel for the web, the hidden rows and columns are not printed. As if you wish to get a print of the worksheet with the concealed columns and rows, you must first unhide them. The absent header titles indicate whether columns or rows are concealed. Here's how to reveal columns or rows:

- Choose the number of headers that will surround the concealed columns or rows. To unhide rows 3 and 6, select each row headers from 2 to 7, for example.

- Select Unhide Rows from the menu when right-clicking the selection (pick Unhide Columns, for columns).

- Select the File tab and then Print from the File menu.

- To get a preview of the print, click Print.

- Make sure that the whole Sheet is chosen in the Print Options box, then click Print.

- The row or column labels do not appear in the print preview or printing.

Get a Print of a workbook: You can just print the worksheet if your MS Excel only includes one spreadsheet. If your workbook includes numerous worksheets, you'll have to go through each one by clicking the tab labeled as sheet and that's how you will print it. Are you unsure whether the workbook contains any concealed worksheets? You can check by following these steps:

- Right-click on any of the sheet tabs.

- The workbook contains one or maybe more concealed worksheets if the Unhide option is present. To reveal the worksheets, click Unhide.

- When you reveal a worksheet by un-hiding it, the worksheet's tab becomes visible. Print the worksheet by selecting the tab of sheet.

Get a Print of a table: You may wish to print just a portion of the worksheet, such as a table. If the table has fewer than ten thousand cells, you will be able to do it in MS Excel. You must use the MS Excel desktop app for spreadsheets with more than ten thousand cells. To print a table, select the very first cell in the table and slide to the final cell to pick all of the cells in the table. If the table contains a number of columns, rather than scrolling, tap on the 1st cell, hold down the shift button then click the final cell.

- To print, go to the File tab and then print.

- If Current Selection isn't already chosen, pick it then click Print option.

- Click Print if you want the preview of the print. If not, then close the display and do all the necessary modifications.

Get a Print of the page numbers present on the worksheet: Excel for the web does not allow you to view, input, or print page numbers. If you are having the MS Excel desktop program, you may add the numbers of page to the worksheet either on the headers (top) or footers (bottom) and get a print. Open the workbook using the Open option in Excel, then in add the page numbers in the page layout and print the spreadsheet from Excel. Here's how to do it:

- Select Open in MS Excel and use the Page Numbers tool to add page numbers to spreadsheets.

- Make a print of the worksheet.

4.8 Collaborate in Excel

Others may use your worksheet if they want to.

- On the ribbon, choose Share, or go to the File tab and then select Share.

Note: If you haven't previously saved your file to One Drive, you will be requested to do so in order to share it.

- From the drop-down menu, choose who you wish to share with, or type an email address or name.

- Optionally, type a message and click Send.

Chapter 5: Detailed Features and Functions of Excel

Microsoft Excel is a widely used Microsoft Office program. It's a spreadsheet tool for saving and analyzing numerical data. In this chapter, we'll go over the most significant features of MS Excel, as well as an explanation about how to use it, its advantages, and other key characteristics. An Excel spreadsheet may be edited and formatted in a variety of ways. Most of the features of Microsoft Excel are discussed here.

5.1 Different Tabs on Main Window

- **Home**: Font size, font color, font styles, background color, formatting choices and styles, alignment, cell insertion and deletion, and editing choices are all included in the home tab.

- **Insert**: It includes options such as table style and format, inserting figures and images, adding graphs and sparklines and charts, equations and symbols and header and footer option.

- **Page Layout**: All Themes, page setup and orientation options are present under this option.

- **Formulas**: As MS Excel can build tables with a big quantity of data, you may use this function to add formulas to the table and receive faster results.

- **Data**: The addition of external data (from the internet), data tools and filtering options are present under this tab.

- **Review**: In the review category, proofreading (like spell check) may be done for an MS excel sheet, and a reader may submit comments in this section.

- **View**: This is where we can change the views in which the spreadsheet is shown. This category contains options for zooming in and out as well as pane arrangement.

5.2 Basics Features

Following are some very basic and useful features of Microsoft Excel.

- **Ribbon:** The MS Excel ribbon includes the tabs on the top of its interface, which helps the users to locate all the commands while using MS Excel.

- **Workbook:** Your Excel file is referred to as a workbook. To start a new Excel workbook, select Blank workbook when you first open the program.

- **Worksheets:** A spreadsheet, also referred to as a worksheet, is a set of cells in which you may store and edit data. Multiple worksheets may be included in an Excel workbook.

- **Format Cells:** You can modify the look of a number without affecting the number itself when you format cells in Excel.

- **Find & Select:** You may use the Find and Replace tool in Excel to rapidly locate and replace specified text. To swiftly select all cells containing formulas, conditional formatting, comments, data validation, constants, and so on, utilize Excel's 'Go To' Special function.

- **Templates:** Instead of starting from scratch, you may use a template to construct an Excel workbook. There are a variety of free templates ready to be utilized.

- **Data Validation:** In Excel, perform data validation to ensure that users input specific values into cells.

- **Print:** By using the print option in Excel, you may print any workbook or worksheet.

- **Share:** Excel data may be shared with Microsoft word files and other documents.

- **Protect:** Create a password-protected Excel file that needs a password to open.

- **Range:** In Excel, a range is a grouping of 2 or more cells.

- **Formulas and Functions:** A formula is a mathematical expression that calculates a cell's value. Functions are pre-programmed formulas that are already present in Excel.

5.3 Data Analysis Tools

Following are some powerful and useful features that Microsoft Excel offers to analyze your data.

- **Sort:** Your Excel data may be sorted by one column or many columns. You have the option of sorting in either descending or ascending order.

- **Filter:** If you only want to see records that fulfill particular criteria, filter your Excel data.

- **Conditional Formatting:** In Excel, conditional formatting allows you to mark cells with a certain color based on their value.

- **Charts:** One simple MS-Excel chart may convey a lot more information than a page of statistics. Making charts is very simple and easy.

- **Pivot tables:** One of MS Excel's most useful features is pivot tables. You may use a pivot table to extract the information from a huge, complex data collection.

- **Tables:** Tables in Excel enable you to rapidly and simply assess your data.

- **What-If Analysis:** This Analysis in MS Excel enables you to experiment with various formula values.

- **Solver:** Excel contains a solver tool that uses operations research approaches to identify optimum solutions to a variety of decision issues.

- **Analysis ToolPak:** This analysis tool s an Excel add-in product that offers financial, engineering data, statistical data analysis capabilities.

5.4 Visual Basic for Applications

Microsoft Excel's VBA (Visual Basic for Applications) refers to the name of Excel's programming language.

- **Develop a Macro:** Excel VBA allows you to automate processes in Excel by creating macros.

- **MsgBox:** In Excel VBA, the MsgBox refers to a dialogue box that you may utilize to educate your program's users.

- **Worksheet and Workbook Objects:** An object in Excel VBA may include another object, which can include another object, and so on. In other words, dealing with this object hierarchy is a part of Excel VBA programming. This may seem confusing at first, but everything is explained further in this chapter. Excel is the most important of all objects. It's referred to as the Application object. Other items are contained inside the application object. The Workbook object, for example (Excel file). This may be any worksheet that you've made. Other objects, like the Worksheet object, are contained inside the Workbook object. Some Other objects, like the Range object, are contained inside the Worksheet object.

- **Range Object:** This object is the most significant object in Excel VBA because it represents a cell (or the cells) on your worksheet.

- **Variables:** Declaring a variable is the process of informing Excel VBA that you are utilizing a variable. Simply put, initializing a variable involves giving it a starting (initial) value.

There are different variables in Excel to execute different tasks,

- Integer variables, for example, are used to hold whole integers.

- Text is stored in string variables.

- A Double variable is more exact than an Integer variable, and it can also hold numbers just after a comma.

- Hold a figure True or False in a Boolean variable.

- **If-Then Statement:** In Excel VBA, utilize the If-Then statement to run code lines if a condition is fulfilled.

- **Loop:** Among the most effective programming methods is looping. With only a few lines of code, you can loop across a number of cells in Excel VBA.

- **Macro Problems and Debugging:** The debugging function in Excel may be used to rectify macro errors.

- **String Manipulation:** Using different Excel VBA procedures, manipulate strings.

- **Date and Time:** Excel VBA allows you to input the date, time, and year.

- **Events:** This feature refers to user-initiated activities that cause Excel VBA to run code.

- **Array:** It is a collection of variables. You may use the array index number and name to refer to a particular variable (element) in an array in Excel VBA.

- **Function and Sub:** A function in Excel VBA can return a value, but a sub cannot.

- **Application Object:** Excel is the parent of all objects. It's referred to as the Application object. The application object allows you to access a variety of Excel-related features.15

- **ActiveX controls:** You can develop controls like command buttons, list boxes, and text boxes, among other things using this feature

- **User form:** You can make an MS Excel VBA User form and use it

Some other incredible features that MS excel have included:

- **Find Duplicates:** This is a useful function. In Excel, look for and highlight duplicate values.

- **Drop-down List:** In Excel, drop-down lists are useful if you want to ensure that users choose from a list rather than inputting their own values.

- **Histogram:** Using this function, you may quickly build a histogram in Excel.

- **Regression:** Using this function, you can perform a linear regression analysis in MS Excel and evaluate the results.

- **Percent Change:** In Excel, the percent change function is often used. To compute a Monthly Change and Total Change, for example.

- **Pareto chart:** IT is a combination of a line graph and column chart. According to the Pareto principle, around 80% of the outcomes arise from 20% of the causes for many events.

- **Loan Amortization Plan:** You may build a loan amortization schedule in Excel using this tool.

- **Random Numbers:** When it comes to producing random numbers, Excel includes two extremely handy tools, which are RAND and RANDBETWEEN.

- **IF function:** It is one of Excel's most often utilized functions. It checks if a condition is fulfilled and returns one figure if true and another figure if false.

- **Lock Cells:** In Excel, you may lock cells to prevent them from being altered.

- **Standard Deviation:** use the STDEV.P function in MS Excel to compute the standard deviation for the total population and the STDEV.S function in MS Excel to determine the standard deviation for a sample.

- **Count Unique Values:** Develop an array formula that counts unique values using this feature.

- **Gantt chart:** Although Gantt is not a chart type in Excel, it is simple to make a Gantt chart by altering the layered bar chart type.

- **CountIF:** Excel's COUNTIF function counts the cells based on a single criterion.

- **Budget:** This tool allows you to construct a budget in Excel.

- **Line Chart:** A line chart is a kind of graph that shows patterns over time. If the horizontal axis has dates, text labels, or a few number labels, use a line chart.

- **Transpose:** To convert columns to rows or rows to columns in Excel, just use the 'Paste Special Transpose' option. The TRANSPOSE feature is also available.

- **Correlation:** To calculate the correlation coefficient among two variables, you can use Excel's Analysis Toolpak add-in or CORREL function.

- **Time Sheet:** In Excel, make a basic timesheet calculator

- **Pie Chart:** these charts are used to show how each value (slice) contributes to a total (pie). One data series is usually used in pie charts.

- **Data Tables:** Rather than generating many scenarios, you can use a data table to experiment with alternative formula values rapidly. A one-variable data table and a two-variable data table may be created.

- **T-Test:** use Excel to execute a t-Test. The t-Test is often used to test the null hypothesis that two population's means are equal.

- **Advanced Filter:** In Excel, Apply the advanced filter to only show records that fulfill a set of complex criteria.

- **Frequency Distribution:** You can quickly construct a frequency distribution in Excel using pivot tables. You may also make a histogram using the Analysis Toolpak.

- **Scatter Plot:** To display scientific XY data, utilize a scatter plot (XY chart). Scatter plots are frequently used to determine if variables X and Y have a connection.

- **ANOVA (analysis of variance)**: in Excel, run a single component ANOVA (analysis of variance). The Null hypothesis, which refers that the means of numerous populations are all equal, is tested using a one-way or single-factor ANOVA.

- **Compare the Two Columns:** In Excel, utilize the IF, MATCH, and ISERROR functions to compare two columns. You may choose whether to show duplicates or unique values.

- **Sumif:** Excel's SUMIF function sums cells depending on a single criterion.

- **Bar Chart:** The horizontal equivalent of a column chart is a bar chart. If you have huge text labels, use a bar chart.

- **Concatenate:** To concatenate (join) strings, use Excel's CONCATENATE function. Just use the '&' operator instead of CONCATENATE if you want.

- **Freeze Panes:** In Excel, if you have a huge table of data, freezing rows or columns might be handy. While navigating through the remainder of the worksheet, you may keep columns or rows displayed.

- **Weighted Average:** In Excel, just use SUM and SUMPRODUCT to compute a weighted average.

- **Delete the Blank Rows:** You can delete any rows with blank cells or blank rows.

- **Sumproduct:** Use Excel's strong SUMPRODUCT function to compute the sum of all the products of related numbers in a single or maybe more range.

- **Percentage:** Using Excel to calculate percentages is simple. The term "percentage" simply means "out of 100," thus 72 percent means "72 out of 100," and 4 percent means "4 out of 100," and so on.

- **Contains Particular Text:** In Excel, utilize ISNUMBER and SEARCH to see whether a cell has specific text. Excel does not have a CONTAINS function.

- **Pmt:** In Excel, the PMT function generates a loan payment based on fixed installments and a fixed interest rate.

- **Compute Age:** In Excel, utilize the functions DATEDIF and TODAY to calculate a person's age. There are three parameters to the DATEDIF function.

- **Goal Seek:** In excel, if you know what formula result you want, use Goal Seek to identify the value that you have to input, which generates that formula result.

- **CAGR:** Excel does not have a CAGR feature. To compute the CAGR (compound annual growth rate) of an investment over a number of years, just utilize the RRI function in Excel.

- **If the Cell is Blank:** In Excel, check if the cell is blank using the IF function with an empty string. To get the same outcome, combine IF and ISBLANK.

- **AverageIf:** Excel's AVERAGEIF function computes the mean of cells that fulfill a set of conditions.

- **Substring:** Excel does not have a SUBSTRING function. To extract substrings in Excel, use the MID, RIGHT, LEFT, FIND, SUBSTITUTE, LEN, REPT, MAX AND TRIM functions.

- **Remove Spaces:** In Excel, the TRIM function eliminates leading spaces, trailing spaces extra spaces, and. To climinate all non-breaking spaces or other spaces, use the SUBSTITUTE function.

- **Move Columns:** In Excel, the shift key is used or the Insert Cut Cells function to move columns. You can also reorder all columns with a single magic move.

- **Check Mark:** In Excel, press SHIFT + P and choose the Wingdings 2 font to add a checkmark symbol. In Excel, you can also create a checkbox.

- **Comparison Operators:** In Excel, compare operators can be used to see whether two numbers are equal, whether one figure is greater than another, and so on.

- **Sparklines:** In Excel, sparklines are the graphs that fit into a single cell. Sparklines are a fantastic way to show patterns.

- **Divide Cells:** Utilize the Text to flash fill, Columns wizard, or formulae to divide the data of a cell into numerous cells.

- **Calendar:** Construct a calendar in MS Excel with 60 days (2021 calendar, 2023 calendar, etc.).

5.5 Formulas and Functions

Excel's bread and butter are formulas and functions. Almost everything fascinating and beneficial you'll ever accomplish in a spreadsheet is driven by them. This chapter presents the fundamental principles you'll need to master Excel formulas and functions. When working with Excel, the terms "formula" and "function" are commonly used interchangeably. They are related, yet they are not identical. A formula is defined as an expression that starts with the equal symbol (=). In contrast, a function is referred to as a formula with a unique name and purpose. In most situations, functions are named for the purpose for which they were created.

Function arguments: To return a result, most functions need inputs. These are referred to as "arguments." The arguments to a function appear within parentheses following the function name, separated by commas. Opening and closing parentheses () are required for all functions.

How to enter a function: Simply start typing if you remember the function's name. The steps are as follows:

- Type the equals symbol (=) and then begin typing. As you write, Excel will generate a list of matching functions.

- Just use arrow keys to choose the specific function you want from the list (or just continue typing).

- To accept a function, press the Tab key. The function will be completed by Excel.

- Enter the required arguments.

- To validate the formula, press Enter.

Combining functions together (nesting): Many Excel formulas have many functions, which may be "nested" within each other. Following are some basic functions you can use in excel:

1. **Date and Time Functions:** Microsoft Excel offers many of the functions to deal with **times** and **dates**.

- **NOW and TODAY:** The TODAY function shows the current date, whereas the NOW function shows the current date and time. The NOW function technically returns the present-day date and time, but also you can format it as only time.

- **DAY, DATE, MONTH and YEAR:** You can break down the date into its basic components using the YEAR, MONTH, and DAY functions, and then reassemble it using the DATE function.

- **HOUR, MINUTE, SECOND, and TIME:** Excel has a variety of time-related parallel functions. You can extract parts of time using the SECOND, MINUTE, and HOUR Functions, and you may construct a TIME from separate components using the TIME function.

2. **Engineering Related Function:**

CONVERT: The majority of engineering functions are rather technical. You'll discover a lot of difficult numeric functions in this area. The CONVERT function, on the other hand, is particularly handy for ordinary unit conversions. You may use CONVERT to convert units of length, weight, temperature, and many other things.

3. Information Functions:

ISBLANK, ISNUMBER, ISERROR, and ISFORMULA:
ISNUMBER, ISLOGICAL, ISTEXT, ISBLANK, ISFORMULA and ISERROR, are just a few of the functions available in Excel for testing the value of a cell. These functions are also known as "IS" functions because they all return FALSE or TRUE depending on the contents of a cell. The ISEVEN and ISODD functions in Excel may be used to determine if a number is even or odd.

4. **Logical Functions:** Many complicated calculations use Excel's logical functions as a foundation. The Boolean variables TRUE and FALSE are returned by logical functions.

- **AND, OR, and NOT:** The base of logical functions of Excel is the **AND function**, the **NOT function**, and the **OR function**.

- **IFERROR and IFNA:** The IFERROR and IFNA functions can be used to capture and handle errors in a direct way. IFERROR function is used to capture any formula error, while IFNA is used to only detect a #N/A error.

- **IF and IFS Functions:** In MS Excel, The IF function is among the most often used functions. To execute more complicated logical checks, several IF functions may be layered together.

5. Reference and Lookup Functions:

- **VLOOKUP and HLOOKUP:** Excel has a variety of functions for looking for and retrieving information. VLOOKUP is the most well-known of them all. HLOOKUP is similar to VLOOKUP. However, it demands data be oriented horizontally.

- **INDEX and MATCH:** INDEX and MATCH provide additional flexibility and power for more intricate lookups. Both the INDEX and MATCH functions are powerful tools that may be used in a variety of formulations.

- **LOOKUP:** When tackling specific issues, the LOOKUP function offers default behavior that makes it beneficial. LOOKUP always makes an approximate match and assumes data are ordered in ascending order. When LOOKUP fails to discover a match, it switches to the next lowest value.

- **ROW and COLUMN:** Column and Row functions can be used to find column and row numbers on a worksheet. If no reference is provided, both COLUMN and ROW return the values for the current cell. Advanced formulas that handle data with comparative row numbers often use the row function.

- **ROWS and COLUMNS:** The ROWS and COLUMNS functions count the number of rows and columns in a reference. A number of data rows in tables, omitting the header row, is returned by ROWS Function.

- **HYPERLINK:** To create a link using a formula, use the HYPERLINK function. It's worth noting that HYPERLINK may be used to create both external and internal linkages.

- **GETPIVOTDATA:** The GETPIVOTDATA function may be used to get data from already existing pivot tables.

- **CHOOSE:** The CHOOSE function comes in help if you need to make a decision based on a set of numbers.

- **TRANSPOSE:** The TRANSPOSE function makes it simple to shift data vertical to horizontal and vice versa.

- **OFFSET:** For all types of dynamic ranges, the OFFSET function comes in handy. It allows you to select a column and row offsets as well as the ultimate column and row size from a starting point. As a consequence, the range can react quickly to changing circumstances and inputs. You may use this range to feed other functions.

- **INDIRECT:** The INDIRECT function enables you to create text references. This notion is a little difficult to grasp initially, but it comes in handy in a variety of scenarios. Each reference has a different dynamic. The reference gets to be updated if the sheet name changes. When columns or rows are added or removed, the INDIRECT function can also be used to "seal" references so that they do not change.

Other complex functions include:

- **STATISTICAL Functions**
- **MATH Functions**
- **TEXT Functions**
- **Dynamic Array functions**

FORMULAS: A formula in MS Excel is a combined expression of different functions that returns a specified result.

How to Enter a Formula: To input a formula, follow these steps:

- Choose a cell.
- Type the equals symbol (=)
- Press enter after typing the formula.

How to Modify a Formula: You have three choices for editing a formula:

- Select the cell and change the formula in the formula bar.
- Edit the cell directly by double-clicking it.
- Select the cell, then press F2, and modify it right away.

- When you're finished, hit Enter to confirm your changes, regardless of which option you choose. Hit the Escape key to cancel the operation and let the formula unchanged.

Order of Operations: Excel follows an "order of operations" sequence when solving a calculation. Any arguments in parentheses must first be evaluated. Excel will then solve exponents if any, which may exist. Excel will conduct multiplication and division after exponents, followed by addition and subtraction. Concatenation will occur after ordinary math operations if the formula requires it. Finally, if logical operators are present, Excel will evaluate them. So the order goes like

1. Use of parentheses

2. Check exponents

3. Division and Multiplication

4. Subtraction and Addition

5. Undergo concatenation

6. Check logical operators

Convert Formulas to Values: Sometimes, you just want to eliminate formulas and replace them with values. In Excel, the simplest method is to simply copy the formula and then paste it using the Paste Special and then Values. This replaces the values returned by the formulas. You may paste data using a keyboard shortcut or the Paste option on the Home tab of the ribbon. Listed below are the most critical and complex Excel formulas a world-class business analyst or top mathematician should know.

1. INDEX MATCH

INDEX MATCH is a formula that combines two Excel functions: INDEX and MATCH.

It is a more advanced version of the HLOOKUP and VLOOKUP formulas (which have some limitations and drawbacks). INDEX-MATCH is a strong Excel formula combination that can help you improve your financial modeling and analysis. INDEX is a table function that returns the data that belongs to the cell depending on the row and column number. MATCH give back the column or row position of a cell.

2. IF combined with OR / AND

A person who has spent a significant amount of time working with different sorts of financial models understands how difficult chained formulas of IF can be. Combining the IF function with the OR the AND function may make calculations simpler to analyze and clear for other people. You can see how the combined separate functions produce a more complicated formula in the example is shown. To produce a result based on two separate integers, you can use the IF and AND functions in Excel. When doing financial modeling and developing conditional scenarios, it may be quite beneficial.

3. OFFSET combined with SUM or AVERAGE

This function isn't complicated, but with the other set of functions, when combined like AVERAGE or SUM, we can produce a quite complex formula. Consider the following scenario: you wish to construct an advanced function which can sum a variety of cells. You can only do a single calculation with the usual SUM formula, but by using OFFSET, cell reference can be shifted around.

Let's see how it works:

For making this specific formula work, use the OFFSET function instead of using the SUM function's ending reference cell. This enables the formula to be dynamic, and you may let Excel know which successive cells you like to combine in the cell. You have some complex Excel formulas now. The OFFSET function belongs to the Excel's Reference and Lookup functions category. A set of cells will be returned by OFFSET. In other words, it will produce a defined number of columns and rows from a given range.

Charts and Pivot Tables arc often used in financial analysis. To ensure that the data source is constantly up to date, the OFFSET function may be used to create a dynamic defined range for charts or pivot tables.

4. XNPV and XIRR

Example of Formula: =XNPV (cash flows, discount rate, dates)

These formulas will come in handy if you work in equity research, investment banking, FP&A (financial planning & analysis tool), as well as any other sector of interlinked finance that needs the discounting cash-flows. Simply said, XIRR and XNPV enable you to assign particular dates to every discounted cash flow. The standard IRR and NPV formulas in Excel have the flaw of assuming that the time intervals between cash flows are equal. With the point of view of an analyst, you'll encounter instances where the cash-flows aren't evenly spaced on a regular basis, and this is the formula that you use to correct it.

5. COUNTIF and SUMIF

Conditional functions are used effectively in both of these functions and they are very advanced formulations. All of the cells which fulfill specified requirements are added in SUMIF, and all of the cells which match specific requirements are counted in COUNTIF. For example, suppose you want to figure out how many bottles of wine you will need for a client event by counting the entire range of cells which are more than the age of 21 or currently 21 years of age (the minimum allowed drinking age by the United States government).

6. IPMT and PMT

Example of Formula: =PMT (# of periods, interest rate, and present value)

You'll need to know these two formulas if you function in real estate, commercial banking, FP&A, or any other financial analyst role that works with the loan schedules. The function of PMT calculates the value of making equal payments throughout the course of a loan's life. You may utilize it in combination with the function of IPMT (which shows you how much interest you'll pay on the same sort of loan) and then separate interest and principal payments.

7. TRIM and LEN

Example of Formula: ==TRIM (text) and LEN (text)

The information we receive is mostly not in a well-organized, and problems such as excess spaces on the start or maybe at the cell's ending line, arises. The LEN function yields the set of entries in a specified text string, which is handy when you need to calculate how many figures are in a text.

8. CONCATENATE

It isn't actually a function in and of itself; it's merely a creative technique of bringing data from separate cells together and making spreadsheets more dynamic. For business analysts undertaking financial modeling, this is an extremely effective tool

9. CELL, MID, LEFT, and RIGHT Functions

The complex Excel functions that are mentioned may be used to generate some really complicated and advanced formulas. The CELL function may return a range of data about a cell's contents (like its location, name, row, or column, and much more). The LEFT command returns the data from the cell's beginning (left side to right side), the MID function delivers text from cell's start point (left side to the right), and the RIGHT function provides text from cell's end (right side to left).

Chapter 6: Guide to Use Excel for Managing Finance

You've come across the perfect book if you need to learn MS Excel for finance. Following are the most significant Excel functions for financial professionals. It is for sure that If you work hard and get through this list, you'll be well on your way to becoming a perfect financial analyst using MS Excel.

6.1 Excel Functions Used For Finance

Here are the most significant functions and formulas you should be familiar with. If you follow this guide, you'll be able to solve any financial issue in Excel. While each one of these formulas and functions is helpful on its own, they could also be combined to create even more powerful formulas and functions.

1. XNPV

Example of Formula: =XNPV (cash-flows, discount-rate, dates)

XNPV has to be the most important Excel formula for financial experts. Any valuation assessment that aims to figure out how much a firm is worth must calculate the NPV (Present Net Value) of a range of cash flows. Unlike Excel's ordinary NPV function, XNPV takes particular dates for the cash flows into account, making it much more helpful and exact.

2. XIRR

Example of Formula: =XIRR (dates, cash-flows)

Another essential function is the XIRR, which estimates the internal charges of return for a sequence of cash flows, given particular dates and is closely connected to XNPV. Because the time intervals among cash flows are unlikely to be precisely the same, XIRR must be used instead of the traditional IRR method.

XIRR vs. IRR in MS Excel

Understanding why utilizing XIRR versus IRR in financial modeling and valuation is crucial. The basic Excel =IRR function might be deceptive because it implies that all time frames in a sequence of cash-flows are equal. This is seldom the case, particularly if you have a large upfront commitment, which nearly never occurs on December 31. XIRR allows you to designate particular dates to every other individual cash flow, which makes the calculation considerably more precise.

3. MIRR

Example of Formula: =MIRR (cost of borrowing, cash-flows, reinvestment rate)

Another noteworthy variance in the internal rate of the return for finance professionals is this. The M in this formula refers to Modified, and it's especially handy when funds from one single investment are put in another. Consider the case when a private company's cash flow is employed in government bonds. If a high-returning firm generates an 18 percent IRR, but the cash is reinvested in an 8 percent bond along the way, the overall IRR will be significantly lower than 18 percent (it will be 15 percent precisely).

4. PMT

Example of Formula: =PMT (number of periods, rate, present value)

For finance experts dealing with real estate's financial modeling, this is a relatively frequent Excel function. The formula may be compared to a calculator of the mortgage payment. You can quickly calculate how much payments will be given an interest rate, the total amount of the debt (e.g., mortgage) and the number of time periods, i.e., years or months, etc. Remember that the total payment includes both the principal and the interest.

5. IPMT

Example of Formula: = IPMT (current period #, rate, present value, total # of periods)

IPMT is a program that calculates the interest component of the fixed debt payment. This Excel function pairs nicely with the PMT function. You may calculate the principal payments for each period by subtracting the interest payment in each month and multiplying the difference between PMT and IMPT.

6. EFFECT

Example of Formula: =EFFECT (# of periods per year, interest rate)

For non-annual compounding, this Excel financial function delivers the actual annual interest rate. For financial professionals, especially those concerned with lending or borrowing, this is a critical Excel function.

7. DB

Example of Formula: =DB (salvage value, cost, current period, life/# of periods)

For accountants and financial experts, this is a fantastic Excel tool. If you don't want to create a big DB (Declining Balance) depreciation module, use this formula in Excel to compute your depreciation expenditure in each period. Analysts generally create a depreciation schedule by hand in financial modeling.

8. RATE

Example of Formula: =RATE (coupon payment per period, # of periods, price of bond, typeface value of bond)

The RATE function may be used to determine a security's Return to Maturity. This is helpful for calculating the average yearly rate of return on a bond purchase.

9. FV

Example of Formula: =FV (# of periods, rate, starting value, payments, type)

If you wish to know that how much money you'll have in the future based on a starting amount, a compounding interest rate, and monthly payments, this function is ideal.

10.   SLOPE

Example of Formula: =SLOPE (independent variable, dependent variable)

When undertaking valuation research and financial modeling, finance professionals often need to determine the Beta (volatility) of the stock. While you can get the Beta of a company from Bloomberg or CapIQ, it's usually preferable to do the study yourself in Excel. Given the returns per weak for the index and stock, you want to compare it to the slope function in MS Excel, which makes it simple to compute Beta.

6.2 Why Build a Financial Model?

Building financial plans is part of everyday life for anybody seeking or furthering a career in investment banking, corporate development, equity research, financial planning and analysis (FP&A), commercial banking, and other fields of corporate finance. Financial models are only tools that assist individuals in making business choices. Whether or not to invest in a firm, security or asset; whether or not to engage in a finance project; whether or not to undertake a merger or acquisition (M&A); and to raise money or not (e.g., perform an IPO) and much more other corporate finance transactions are all examples of these choices.

The financial model enables decision-makers to run scenarios, examine possible results, and, ideally, make an educated choice. There is a lot of discussion regarding software applications that may be employed, but the reality is that Excel is utilized for the great majority of financial modeling.

6.3 Excel Tips and Tricks

Excel is the most used financial modeling program used by banks, businesses, and organizations. The key reason for this is Excel's incredible adaptability. Excel is a blank slate that can be completely modified and suited to the scenario for any business or investment opportunity. But at the other hand, there are no checks or regulations in place to verify that the model is reliable and error-free. For this financial modeling guide, below are some of the most crucial Excel tips:

- Make use of as many shortcuts of a keyboard as you can.

- Make formulas and computations as easy as possible by breaking them into smaller chunks.

- Use the grouping option to structure the financial model's parts.

- To easily discover all hardcoded formulas and numbers, use F5 to (go to special).

- Audit the model using Trace Dependents and Trace Precedents.

- Apply specified dates to the cash-flows using XNPV and XIRR.

- When searching up the information, use INDEX MATCH rather than VLOOKUP. 8. To make dates dynamic, use a mixture of IF statements and date functions (EOMONTH) and

- When presenting or distributing the financial model, remove the gridlines.

- Learn all of the most significant Excel formulas for financial modeling and memories them.

6.4 Financial Modeling Best Practices

Analysts that succeed in financial modeling succeed at structuring and arranging their spreadsheets in addition to having strong Excel abilities. Here are the top ten recommended practices for model structure:

- Color-code inputs and formulas to differentiate them (e.g., black and blue)

- Create a three-statement model on a single worksheet (do not divide the assertions into separate pages).

- Make the drivers and assumptions stand out from the other model (one of the section on the top)

- To easily separate parts, use distinct headings and subheads (with strong shading).

- To express assumptions or calculations that need to be explained, utilize the cell comments feature (shift + F2).

- Include error checks, such as guaranteeing that the balance sheet would be balancing (without the need of a "plug").

- Bring forward (or repeat) information that aids consumers in understanding the model's rationale

- Unless absolutely required, avoid connecting to other Excel spreadsheets (and if you have to do so, indicate the links that exist clearly.)

- Only utilize circular references if absolutely essential (and use the iterative computation to solve them)

- To summarize key information, use charts, tables and graphs.

6.5 Building the Forecast

The "art" of financial modeling is primarily concerned with creating assumptions about the business's future performance. It is the most sensitive and crucial aspect of a company's value.

This guide will cover a variety of forecasting methods, including:

- **A top-down approach.** You will start from the TAM (Total addressable market) and work your way down depending on market segmentation and share such as geography, goods, and consumers until you reach revenue.

- **A bottom-up approach**. In the situation of an e-commerce firm, this strategy starts with the most fundamental drivers of the company, such as then conversion rate, website traffic, order value, and lastly, revenue.

- **Regression analysis.** This sort of prediction uses regression analysis in MS Excel to examine the link between the business's income and other variables such as marketing expenditure and product pricing.

- **Year-over-year growth rate.** This is the simplest kind of predicting. Simply use a percentage growth rate year over year (YoY).

Conclusion

Microsoft Excel is the world's most well-known and widely used spreadsheet application. This program, which was first released by Microsoft in the year 1987, has seen several improvements over the years, which makes it the go-to solution for spreadsheet editing and graphing.

Among other things, there are apps, macro programming pivot tables. Millions of people use this program on a regular basis on all online browsers, which includes Android, Windows, iOS and macOS. Excel has been part of the MS Office suite since 1990, a collection of presentation, document, and email editing tools that serve a wide range of usage scenarios in a contemporary collaborative work environment. The latest Excel versions provide everything you'll need to get started with and progress as an expert, as well as a slew of additional useful features. Microsoft 2021 brings a lot of new changes and upgrades, the most prominent of which is the idea that Excel will be finally available as part of the subscription plan. As a result, although changes used to happen every few years, you can now expect them every day. MS Excel recognizes and organizes patterns and data, allowing you to save time. Create spreadsheets quickly and effortlessly using templates or from scratch, and then use current features to do computations. You may exchange documents using Microsoft 365 on Excel. Workbooks may be shared with others as you work on new versions, and real-time synchronization allows you to finish tasks quickly. It encompasses both basic and specialized technologies that may be found in practically every sector. The Excel spreadsheet allows you to quickly and easily generate, display, update, and share data with others. When reading and altering excel files linked to emails, you can create spreadsheets, data tables, data reports, and budgets. If you get more acquainted with different definitions, you will be able to understand the most up-to-date features and tools that MS Excel has to offer. The truth is that Excel's capabilities can help you meet practically any personal or business need. All you should do is commit your time and abilities. Although many skills have a long learning curve, with practice and time, you will notice that some skills become second nature. And anyway, it is through practice that a man improves. And after all, no other tech competitor has such optional tools and a consistent experience. As a result, Microsoft Excel is the greatest tool for you to get your job done quickly.

Microsoft Excel is, without a doubt, a challenging application to grasp and operate. That's why it is frequently advisable to enlist the help of others in figuring out how to cope with it efficiently. If you are a student who needs to know how to utilize Microsoft Excel to finish a school assignment, a businessperson who wants to expand their experience and learn new skills, or a person who wants to get a basic knowledge of Excel

Spreadsheets for personal use, this book is appropriate for you. You may get a lot of high-quality visuals, tips, and techniques by going through this Microsoft Excel guide. You'll also get a comprehensive overview of all Excel essentials, allowing you to work with Microsoft Excel more comfortably on a daily basis. So you should give a chance to this book since it has all of the important facts.

www.ingramcontent.com/pod-product-compliance
Lightning Source LLC
LaVergne TN
LVHW022322060326
832902LV00020B/3609